THE 70th WEEK
OF DANIEL

THE 70th WEEK OF DANIEL

God's Wrath Poured Out

M.D. SPARR

Trilogy Christian Publishers

A Wholly Owned Subsidiary of Trinity Broadcasting Network

2442 Michelle Drive

Tustin, CA 92780

For information, address Trilogy Christian Publishing

Rights Department, 2442 Michelle Drive, Tustin, Ca 92780.

Trilogy Christian Publishing/ TBN and colophon are trademarks of Trinity Broadcasting Network.

For information about special discounts for bulk purchases, please contact Trilogy Christian Publishing.

Trilogy Disclaimer: The views and content expressed in this book are those of the author and may not necessarily reflect the views and doctrine of Trilogy Christian Publishing or the Trinity Broadcasting Network.

10 9 8 7 6 5 4 3 2 1

Library of Congress Cataloging-in-Publication Data is available.

ISBN 979-8-89041-873-9

ISBN 979-8-89041-874-6 (ebook)

ACKNOWLEDGMENTS

In pursuing my studies of the "rapture" and the "last days" over the last decade, I must acknowledge and thank the pastors and theologians who have been instrumental in my understanding of eschatology through their teachings on the Scriptures. They would include, but not limited to pastors and theologians: Chuck Smith, Jack Hibbs, Amir Tsarfati, Barry Stagner, Dr. Rick Yohn, Allen Nolen, Paul LeBoutillier, John Brown, David Jones, and Jan Markell, as well as the works of C. H. Spurgeon, John F. Walvoord, Joseph Seiss, Merrill C. Tenney, Donald Grey Barnhouse, Matthew Henry, and Henry Alford.

I dedicate this book to my lovely wife, Victoria. Her unwavering devotion and encouragement have inspired me to delve deeper into God's Word, and I am truly grateful to our God in Heaven for bringing us together.

Thank you, Vickie, I will always love you.

TABLE OF CONTENTS

PREFACE

The 70th Week of Daniel: God's Wrath Poured Out is an easy-to-read study of the seven-year tribulation as written in the book of Revelation. I aimed to create an engaging, easy-to-follow guide through the tribulation to encourage readers to choose Christ as Lord and Savior and to strengthen those who already know Him. I pray that as you read this book, the love of Christ surrounds you and brings clarity to the "seventieth-week" vision given by God to the prophet Daniel and as revealed to the apostle John by Jesus Christ. We will study the book of Revelation, as it describes the seven-year tribulation, God's wrath, the reign of the antichrist, and the second coming of Jesus Christ. May God bless you with wisdom as we journey through Daniel's seventieth week.

Thank you all for your devotion to God's Word.

M. D. Sparr

Ordained in 2005 through
United Christian Faith Ministries.

ACS, Sure Foundation Theological Institute, 2005.

PROLOGUE: THE ONSET OF THE TRIBULATION

Now the word of the LORD came to me, saying, "Son of man, set your face against Gog, of the land of Magog, the prince of Rosh, Meshech, and Tubal, and prophesy against him, and say, 'Thus says the Lord GOD: "Behold, I am against you, O Gog, the prince of Rosh, Meshech, and Tubal. I will turn you around, put hooks into your jaws, and lead you out, with all your army, horses, and horsemen, all splendidly clothed, a great company with bucklers and shields, all of them handling swords. Persia, Ethiopia, and Libya are with them, all of them with shield and helmet; Gomer and all its troops; the house of Togarmah from the far north and all its troops—many people are with you.

"Prepare yourself and be ready, you and all your companies that are gathered about you; and be a guard for them. After many days you will be visited. In the latter years you will come into the land of those brought back from the sword and gathered from many people on the mountains of Israel, which had long been desolate; they were brought out of the nations, and now all of them dwell safely."''

Ezekiel 38:1–8

In chapter 38 of the book of Ezekiel, we have the prophetic message of the "Gog and Magog" war against Israel. There is much speculation between Bible scholars regarding who Gog is and which cities or countries Magog represents. Most agree that Gog is the leader of Rosh, Meshech, and Tubal, and Magog is the coalition of countries who join with Gog to come against Israel. However, there is some disagreement among them regarding which modern-day countries are now being called, compared to what they were called in the days of Ezekiel when the prophecy speaks of Rosh, Meshech, and Tubal. Many believe Rosh to be Russia, Meshech to be Moscow, and Tubal to be the city of Tobolsk. They consider Meshech and Tubal the two modern cities within Russia that we are familiar with today. However, Tubal in Ezekiel's time may have been closer to modern-day Turkey. However, there is nothing in Scripture to confirm all the countries which may be involved. It's all open to interpretation because of some changes over the centuries in geographical boundaries and the names being different in the past. Within the entire prophetic chapter, it also lists other nations, such as Iran, Turkey, Libya, and Ethiopia, who will ally with Russia to attack Israel. Ethiopia (which used to be Cush) is south of Egypt and is known today as Sudan. Most biblical scholars today agree that the countries of Russia, Iran, Turkey, Libya, and Ethiopia are the main players in this war since the country of the north would most likely be modern-day Russia, who will lead the others to join with him as allies to attack Israel. I've mentioned this prophecy here now because it does have some relationship to the timeline of the tribulation. Some scholars believe it will occur just before the tribulation, some believe it will happen in the middle of the tribulation, and some believe it will occur at the end. Still, others say it is the same Gog and Magog war that occurs at the end of the millennial reign of Christ when Satan is released, as we see in chapter 20, verse 8 of Revelation. While Scripture calls both Gog and Magog, they are two distinctly different wars made up of different players a thousand years apart. The Gog and Magog mentioned in the book of Ezekiel refer to an army of men led by a powerful human leader. However, in the book of Revelation, the "Gog" mentioned in chapter 20 is Satan himself, who will deceive nations and lead them into a war against Jesus and His saints after his release from bondage. "Gog and Magog" are spiritual terms that could apply to any powerful leader who would lead many nations into battle to conquer. It was commonly used to describe the raiding armies of the north, who were known for their ferocity as warriors and were often considered barbaric. Gog would describe the ruthless leader of these armies, and Magog would describe the armies or nations. The term is used in Scripture much like Mystery Babylon was used to describe any nation similar to the wickedness of the physical city of Babylon from Genesis chapter 11. In Genesis chapter 10, Magog is mentioned for the first time as the name of one of Japheth's sons, who was a son of Noah. Magog and his clan settled in the Northern lands above Israel, close to what we call Russia today. His descendants became feared barbarian warriors in ancient times, thus coining the term for warring nations. Ezekiel's "Gog" occurs before the onset of the tribulation around the time of the rapture. Humanity may only find the details out when it is the proper time for the prophecies to be fulfilled. But we do have scriptural evidence in the following prophetic truths:

An influential leader, "Gog," who rules over "Magog," will come from the area north of Israel, who has never come against Israel before, and lead a coalition of allied nations against them (Ezekiel 38:1–6).

The allied nations will come from many areas surrounding Israel, including Iran, Turkey, Libya, Ethiopia, and possibly some regions of Europe (Ezekiel 38:1–6).

Gog's forces will come against Israel as a great, powerful, and heavily armed militia (Ezekiel 38:4– 6).

It will occur in the "last days," far from Ezekiel's time

(Ezekiel 38:8).

This leader will be driven by his evil plans and pulled by God to act on them (Ezekiel 38:10).

Gog will attack Israel when they are enjoying ample safety within their land (Ezekiel 38:8).

Gog will attack Israel when they are gathered back to their land, which started when Israel became a Nation on May 14, 1948 (Ezekiel 38:8, 12).

Gog will attack Israel when they are prospering (Ezekiel 38:12–13).

Other nations will watch and scheme to see how Gog's conquest of Israel might benefit or disadvantage them; however, none will come to their aid (Ezekiel 38:12–13).

The Lord of Hosts will defend Israel and defeat Gog to glorify Himself among all the nations (Ezekiel 38:16).

The war that the world has recently witnessed in Israel since its beginning on October 7, 2023, and is in progress at the writing of this book closely resembles the Gog and Magog war; however, it is not. Although it involves some countries mentioned in the prophecy, it does not have all the key players. According to news outlets, terrorists sponsored by Iran attacked them, and there is some speculation of Russian involvement. Still, unlike the biblical conflict of Ezekiel, this conflict also has some aid from the United States, whereas no country comes to the help of Israel in the Ezekiel prophecy. It does, however, show us the signs of wars and rumors of wars, warned by Jesus, which have escalated now in the end times we are living, and it could be the beginning of events that will build up to the prophetic war. Though the Gog and Magog war of Ezekiel will occur before the onset of the tribulation, we do not know if this war will occur after or before the rapture of the church. The church may or may not witness the beginning of this war. If we do, look up, for your redemption is near.

The New Testament has many scriptures that tell the church we are to expect tribulation in the world. Jesus told His disciples, "In the world you will have tribulation" (John 16:33). In Acts 14:22, Paul, in his ministry, said, "We must through many tribulations enter the kingdom of God." Scriptural references that Christians would have to endure tribulations are also found in Romans chapters 8 and 12, 2 Corinthians 1 and 7, Ephesians 3, 2 Thessalonians 1, and Revelation 1 and 2, but they were referring to general tribulations that come upon us in our lives as Christians. In John 15:18, Jesus told us, "If the world hates you, you know that it hated Me before it hated you." Many followers of Christ are enduring tribulation as they are being severely persecuted around the world today. Some say it won't be long until the governments of the free world may also begin to persecute Christians severely. We will all have to endure these tribulations occasionally in our walk with Jesus. The Bible teaches us, however, that there will come a time in the future of a great tribulation that will be unprecedented and will eclipse these more minor tribulations that we endure today. In his book *The Rapture Question*, Theologian John F. Walvoord writes,

> This future time of trouble, according to scripture, will concern three classes of people:
>
> The nation of Israel.
>
> The pagan Gentile world.
>
> The saints or elect who will live in that time of trouble.
>
> It is of utmost significance that every scripture describing the participants in this future tribulation

period refers to Israelites as Israelites, Gentiles as Gentiles, and the saints as saints without ever once using any of the distinctive terms that apply to believers in this present age. The tribulation passages in the Old and New Testaments further illustrate that there is a twofold purpose in the time of great tribulation: (1) to bring to conclusion "the times of the Gentiles" (Luke 21:24); (2) to prepare for the restoration and the regathering of Israel in the millennial reign of Christ following the Second Advent.

The tribulation will not be for any purpose concerning the body of Christ who is on earth before the onset of the tribulation. It has no purpose in disciplining believers because it is not about the church. The church will be in heaven with Jesus during the tribulation. The time of the tribulation is for the Gentiles who have rejected Christ and for Israel's regathering. Its purpose is to punish those who have taken the "mark" during the antichrist's reign. These are the people who worship the antichrist and will persecute and murder God's people as his pawns. Its primary purpose will be to awaken Israel to the realization that Jesus, their Messiah, had already come as a suffering servant, bringing them to mourn for the One whom they pierced. In this, the prophecy of Zechariah 12:10–14 will be fulfilled, and also the promise of Romans 11:26. The Jewish people will cry out to Jesus in repentance, mourning their past rejection of Him, and God will secure their salvation. Theologian C.H. Spurgeon wrote,

> We know of a surety, because God has said it, that the Jews will be restored to their own land, and that they shall inherit the goodly country which the Lord has given unto their fathers by a covenant of

salt forever; but, better still, they shall be converted to the faith of our Lord Jesus Christ, and shall see in him the house of David restored to the throne of Israel.

"The seven-year tribulation" and "the great tribulation" are terms used to describe the final seven-year period during the "end times" as laid out in the book of Revelation. This period will lead to the second coming of Christ and the final battle of Armageddon. These two events will occur just before Jesus begins His rule on earth as Lord of lords and King of kings, to reign with His saints in the millennial kingdom. The "great tribulation" more commonly refers to the final three-and-a-half years of the tribulation, although the phrase "great tribulation" is only used once in the entire book of Revelation. The tribulation period is known as the "day of the Lord" or "Daniel's seventieth week," written in Daniel chapter 9, the final seven years of the world, beginning with a covenant between Israel and the antichrist. After these seven years, under the antichrist's rule, Jesus will establish His kingdom and rule on earth for one thousand years (the millennial kingdom). The "seventieth week of Daniel" is the seven-year tribulation. Daniel's vision of "seventy-sevens" in the prophecy is seventy times seven years, totaling 490 years. One prophetic "week" equals one "seven-year" period. So, the seventieth week of Daniel is the final seven-year period during the "last days" according to his prophetic vision. These seven years are what we refer to as the tribulation or the great tribulation.

The prophecy's first "sixty-nine weeks" have already occurred, leading to the Messiah Jesus' triumphal entry into Jerusalem. These sixty-nine weeks encompass the timespan between the commandment to restore and rebuild Jerusalem and the triumphal entry. Four hundred and eighty-three years after Artaxerxes gave the commandment to Nehemiah to restore and rebuild the city of Jerusalem, Jesus fulfilled this prophecy on the exact day as was given to Daniel. According to the prophecy given to Daniel in his prophetic vision from God, Jesus rode into Jerusalem and declared Himself as the Messiah precisely 483 years after Artaxerxes issued the commandment mentioned in Daniel 9:25, which was written as "seven weeks and sixty-two weeks." All that is left to be fulfilled in Daniel's prophecy now is the final or seventieth week of Daniel. According to the signs from Jesus' discourse to His disciples in Matthew chapter 24 (the Olivet Discourse), we live in the "end times" today. The onset of the tribulation could happen sooner than we may all think. When Jesus spoke of "this generation" that "will by no means pass away till all these things take place" in Matthew 24:34, He spoke of Israel being established again as a nation. David Ben-Gurion, head of the Jewish Agency in 1948, proclaimed the establishment of the State of Israel, and US President Harry S. Truman recognized the new nation on the same day, which took place on May 14, 1948. The prophecy of Jesus and Isaiah has been fulfilled; a nation was born at once in one day. Jesus spoke of Israel becoming a nation and flourishing in Matthew 24:32. He tells the parable of the fig tree just before He speaks about the "last generation." In the New Testament, "fig" or "fig tree" is used in parables to refer to Israel, as it does here in Jesus' parable given in His discourse on the mount of olives. Today, many Jewish people have returned to their "promised land" from all parts of the world, and it is flourishing as a nation. The prophecy is written in Isaiah chapter 66: "Who has heard such a thing? Who has seen such things? Shall the earth be made to give birth in one day? Or shall a nation be born at once? For as soon as Zion was in labor, She gave birth to her children."

Here is Daniel's seventy-weeks prophecy as written in chapter 9 of the book of Daniel:

Seventy weeks are determined For your people and

for your holy city, To finish the transgression, To make an end of sins, To make reconciliation for iniquity, To bring in everlasting righteousness, To seal up vision and prophecy, And to anoint the Most Holy. Know therefore and understand, That from the going forth of the command To restore and build Jerusalem Until Messiah the Prince, There shall be seven weeks and sixty-two weeks; The street shall be built again, and the wall, Even in troublesome times. And after the sixty-two weeks Messiah shall be cut off, but not for Himself; And the people of the prince who is to come Shall destroy the city and the sanctuary. The end of it shall be with a flood, And till the end of the war desolations are determined. Then he shall confirm a covenant with many for one week; But in the middle of the week He shall bring an end to sacrifice and offering. And on the wing of abominations shall be one who makes desolate, Even until the consummation, which is determined, Is poured out on the desolate.

Daniel 9:24–27

Following the sixty-nine weeks of Daniel's prophecy and leading up to the seventieth week of Daniel, we have the period of the church age, a two-thousand-year gap between the end of the sixty-nine weeks and the start of the seventieth. In our present time, the "church age" is about to end, and the fullness of the Gentiles will come to fruition (Romans 11:25). God chose not to give Daniel a prophetic vision of the church age itself, which accounts for the two-thousand-year "gap" in the timeline of the prophecy. The final week of Daniel's prophetic vision is the seven-year tribulation that leads to Christ's return. He will establish His rule and reign with His saints on earth for a thousand years. The seven-year tribulation, as presented in the book of Revelation, will show both physical events taking place in this realm and spiritual events taking place concurrently in the spiritual realm.

In our present time, no other biblical event needs to occur before the "catching up" or rapture of the church from the earth. We know it is imminent, but "no one knows the day or the hour," so the church, also referred to as the *bride*, endures patiently now, eagerly awaiting the return of the *bridegroom*, Jesus Christ. When the Father deems it is time, Jesus will race back to receive His bride, the church, and we will be "caught up" to Him in the air and then go on with Him into heaven. All who place their trust and faith in the gospel of Jesus Christ become "born-again" by faith and become a part of the body of Christ, known as the "church" and often referred to as the "bride" in Scripture. The apostle Paul considered in his time that the rapture event was imminent, and he taught this in his epistles. John F. Walvoord wrote the following in his book *The Rapture Question*:

> The nature of the Tribulation is also one of practical importance. If the church is destined to endure the persecutions of the Tribulation, it is futile to proclaim the coming of the Lord as an imminent hope. Instead, it should be recognized that Christ cannot come until these predicted sorrows have been accomplished. On the other hand, if Christ will come for His church before the predicted time of trouble, Christians can regard His coming as an imminent daily expectation. From a practical standpoint, the doctrine has tremendous implications.

Since Jesus said no one knows the day or hour, only the Father knows (Matthew 24:36, Mark 13:32), it brings light to the question of imminency. If Christians in their sinful flesh knew the exact day or hour that the Lord would come for them, then some might not stay ready while abiding in Christ in anticipation of His imminent return. Instead, they might revel in their fleshly desires until the last moment instead of *occupying* until His return. We, as Christians, have been instructed by Jesus to abide in Him and spread the good news of the gospel to those lost in the world. How many lost souls would be saved if imminency was not in place? It is easy for mankind to follow his sinful desires; staying on the narrow path and abiding in Christ is difficult. Christians must work at it, enduring and resisting temptation daily. Without the imminency of Christ's return, people, in general, knowing when the appearance of Jesus would take place, would follow the world until the appointed time. They would know when He was coming!

For this reason, God didn't want the time of Jesus' return for His bride to be known. If you look at the passages of Luke 17:22–37, it describes the rapture in the first passages (26–30). The description reads as follows:

> And as it was in the days of Noah, so it will be also in the days of the Son of Man: They ate, they drank, they married wives, they were given in marriage, until the day that Noah entered the ark, and the flood came and destroyed them all. Likewise as it was also in the days of Lot: They ate, they drank, they bought, they sold, they planted, they built; but on the day that Lot went out of Sodom it rained fire and brimstone from heaven and destroyed them all. Even so will it be in the day when the Son of Man is revealed.

In simpler terms, life continued as usual until Noah was safely locked in the ark, and the angel of the Lord rescued

Lot out of Sodom. God is good at saving His own before unleashing His wrath. However, in verse 33 of Luke chapter 17, Jesus moves away from the subject of the rapture to describe "the tribulation" in the final passages (33–36). The rapture of believers will be similar to the events of Noah entering the ark and Lot leaving Sodom in this way: the faithful will be taken out of harm's way just before God's wrath is unleashed, starting with the opening of the seven seals.

Paul, in 2 Thessalonians 2:8, tells us that the "lawless one" cannot be revealed until the restraining force of the Holy Spirit, who lives within all believers who comprise the church, is taken out of the way. This event is commonly known as the rapture. The Restrainer steps aside when the church has been caught up to Jesus in the air. As Christians, we've been sealed by the Holy Spirit until the redemption of our bodies; thus, the church must be removed before God's wrath to take He who restrains out of the way (2 Thessalonians 2:7). In Revelation 4:1, the apostle John is called by God to "come up here." The Lord then reveals to him the "things which must take place." I believe it is at this point in Revelation chapter 4 that the future rapture of the church takes place and that the "trumpet" in this verse is the same trumpet described in 1 Thessalonians 4:16. The church of Christ must be gone before the antichrist enters the world according to God's Word. We also know that there must be an interval between the rapture of the bride and the second coming of Christ for the marriage of the Lamb and the marriage supper to take place before we, the saints, follow our Lord and King back to the earth from heaven at the second coming. Also, if we are told in 1 Thessalonians 4:18, "to encourage one another with these words," then how encouraging would it be if we, the church, were all beat up during the tribulation before the rapture event takes place? The following scriptures clearly show the church will be removed from harm before the wrath of God is unleashed:

"Because you have kept My command to persevere, I also will keep you from the hour of trial which shall come upon the whole world, to test those who dwell on the earth" (Revelation 3:10).

"And to wait for his Son from heaven, whom he raised from the dead, even Jesus who delivers us from wrath to come" (1 Thessalonians 1:10).

"For God did not appoint us to wrath, but to obtain salvation through our Lord Jesus Christ" (1 Thessalonians 5:9).

"Much more then, having now been justified by His blood, we shall be saved from wrath through Him" (Romans 5:9).

> And now you know what is restraining, that he may be revealed in his own time. For the mystery of lawlessness is already at work; only He who now restrains will do so until He is taken out of the way. And then the lawless one will be revealed, whom the Lord will consume with the breath of His mouth and destroy with the brightness of His coming.
>
> 2 Thessalonians 2:6–8

"Then we who are alive and remain shall be caught up together with them in the clouds to meet the Lord in the air. And thus we shall always be with the Lord. Therefore comfort one another with these words" (1 Thessalonians 4:17–18).

"After these things I looked, and behold, a door standing open in heaven. And the first voice which I heard was like a trumpet speaking with me, saying, 'Come up here, and I will show you things which must take place after this'" (Revelation 4:1).

The rapture is all about resurrection and translation, depending on whether you're "asleep" in Christ or "alive" in Christ when it takes place. Here is an explanation of the resurrections.

According to Jesus, there are two resurrections: (1) the resurrection of life and (2) the resurrection of condemnation.

(1) The resurrection of life (first resurrection) consists of "two parts": There is a resurrection at the beginning of the tribulation (rapture) and a resurrection at the end of the tribulation, just before the millennium. The second part of the resurrection of life is for those who died in Christ during the tribulation. These will be resurrected and joined with the saints who were raptured before the beginning of the tribulation.

(2) The resurrection of condemnation (second resurrection) will occur just before the great white throne judgment (immediately after the millennium), where the condemned will be judged on their own merits without Jesus and thrown into the lake of fire.

We also see no mention of the church in Revelation chapters 6 through 19. I see this as further validation that the rapture must happen before the onset of the seven-year tribulation, which begins shortly after the time of the release of the first horseman in Revelation 6:2. This is the beginning of "God's wrath" being unleashed onto the world, with the judgments steadfastly increasing in severity and purpose as they progress.

Although many scholars disagree on the timing of the rapture event, many must ignore some scriptures to validate their beliefs. As always, a student of Scripture must rely entirely on the help of the Holy Spirit to discern what is truth. It is essential to pray continuously for wisdom and discernment and to be filled with the Holy Spirit. Lean on the Lord and walk in the Spirit, not in the flesh.

Once the church is safe with the Lord, and the "Restrainer" is taken out of the way, the seven-year tribulation (seventieth week of Daniel) will begin. After the rapture, the "lawless one" will appear on the scene, and soon after that, he will sign a seven-year peace covenant with Israel. This covenant will occur when Jesus opens the first of the seven seals, and the rider of the white horse appears in chapter 6 of Revelation. The white horseman represents the antichrist or "lawless one" mentioned in 2 Thessalonians chapter 2, who will rise out of the world's nations. The antichrist is the embodiment of Satan, but the world will perceive him as a charismatic "man of peace" and a brilliant political leader. It is at this point that the tribulation begins. Once the seven-year covenant of peace with Israel is signed, the world will embrace him as a savior to their problems. At the midpoint of the tribulation, after the first three-and-a-half years, the antichrist will deceitfully break his agreement with Israel, and it will begin the satanic oppression against the Jews and the Christians. The "abomination of desolation" occurs when the antichrist declares himself in the temple as being God. Satan will show his power and release his wrath against God's people, and God's wrath will escalate at this point as it leads up to the second coming of Christ. Now, we can start our journey through the seventieth week of Daniel.

CHAPTER 1

THE LAMB OPENS THE SEALS

And I saw in the right hand of Him who sat on the throne a scroll written inside and on the back, sealed with seven seals. Then I saw a strong angel proclaiming with a loud voice, "Who is worthy to open the scroll and to loose its seals?" And no one in heaven or on the earth or under the earth was able to open the scroll, or to look at it.

So I wept much, because no one was found worthy to open and read the scroll, or to look at it. But one of the elders said to me, "Do not weep. Behold, the Lion of the tribe of Judah, the Root of David, has prevailed to open the scroll and to loose its seven seals."

And I looked, and behold, in the midst of the throne and of the four living creatures, and in the midst of the elders, stood a Lamb as though it had been slain, having seven horns and seven eyes, which are the seven Spirits of God sent out into all the earth. Then He came and took the scroll out of the right hand of Him who sat on the throne.

Revelation 5:1–7

The "Seal" Judgments

We see God the Father on the throne, holding a seven-sealed scroll. John is asked, "Who is worthy?" Then, he is told that no one in heaven nor on earth was able to open the scroll. John begins to weep deeply, and then he hears, "Behold, the Lion of the tribe of Judah, the Root of David, has prevailed to open the scroll and to loose its seven seals." Only the Son, Jesus the Lamb who was slain, was worthy enough to open the scroll. John looked and heard, "Behold, in the midst of the throne and of the four living creatures, and in the midst of the elders, stood a Lamb as though it had been slain, having seven horns and seven eyes, which are the seven Spirits of God sent out into all the earth. Then He came and took the scroll out of the right hand of Him who sat on the throne."

When we study the book of Revelation, we must realize that only some passages are in chronological order. However, the seal, trumpet, and bowl judgments do take place in the order they are described. So, when you see the "beast" coming up in Revelation chapter 13, it is not the point in time chronologically that the lawless one is revealed. The antichrist comes onto the scene before chapter 13. The son of perdition appears in Revelation chapter 6 when the first of the four horsemen is released. Revelation chapter 13 will give a more descriptive representation of his character when we get there. Now here, as the first seal is being opened, he is introduced into the world as the rider of the white horse carrying a "bow" (Revelation 6:2). This is when the lawless one comes into worldview, and the seventieth week of Daniel will shortly follow. At this point in Revelation, the antichrist makes his first appearance and brings a covenant with Israel, symbolized by the "bow" held by the rider of the white horse. Satan controls the antichrist, but when he first makes himself known, he will deceptively appear as a "man of peace," just as Satan sometimes appears as "an angel of light." Some have claimed that this first horseman could be Jesus the King because this first rider is on a white horse and wearing a crown. But this rider is not the Lord. In the scripture, the Greek word used for "bow" is the same word used in the Greek translation of the Old Testament (the Septuagint) for the word "rainbow" as described in Genesis 9:13. This was where God gave the rainbow as a symbol of the covenant that He made with all the earth not to destroy it with a flood ever again. Therefore, the bow is representative of a covenant (in this case, between the antichrist and Israel), which the rider of the white horse arrives carrying. The Greek word in this verse for the "crown" he is wearing is of a conqueror, not a king. This crown and the rider's bow signify that he is the lawless one, not Jesus. In Revelation chapter 19, Jesus also appears on a white horse with a sword and wearing the royal crowns of victory, distinguishing Him from the "lawless one."

> Now I saw when the Lamb opened one of the seals; and I heard one of the four living creatures saying with a voice like thunder, "Come and see." And I looked, and behold, a white horse. He who sat on it had a bow; and a crown was given to him, and he went out conquering and to conquer.

Revelation 6:1–2

The Lamb has opened the first seal, and the antichrist has arrived on the world scene. The four horsemen of the apocalypse (which means the revealing) are "symbols" that represent the horrors that will plague the earth and its people during these times of the tribulation. It's important to note that these are not real horsemen who have been set free into the world. The first horseman represents a natural person who comes to conquer the hearts of men; however, the other horsemen are symbols that represent judgments being unleashed onto the world and its people. Other than the first horseman, the other three have distinct "characteristics" defining the judgments of God.

> When He opened the second seal, I heard the second living creature saying, "Come and see." Another horse, fiery red, went out. And it was granted to the one who sat on it to take peace from the earth, and that people should kill one another; and there was given to him a great sword.
>
> Revelation 6:3–4

Now, Jesus continues opening the seals. The "second seal" unleashes a "fiery red" horse, whose rider will end any aspect of peace on the earth and cause people to kill one another. The rider carries a sword in his hand. Two Greek words describe swords, one being for a large sword used in battle (*rhomphaia*), and is like the sword protruding from the mouth of Jesus as He comes to strike down the nations in Revelation 19:15. The other word for sword (*machaira*) is what is used here in this scripture, which describes a short sword or dagger. It is the dagger that this rider holds, and it indicates anarchy, civil unrest, and the unwarranted killing of one another. Without the restraining force of the Spirit-filled church on the earth, humanity will begin to kill each other in large numbers for personal gain, survival, and just for the thrill of killing. The world will soon witness a much more significant surge in lawlessness.

> When He opened the third seal, I heard the third living creature say, "Come and see." So I looked, and behold, a black horse, and he who sat on it had a pair of scales in his hand. And I heard a voice in the midst of the four living creatures saying, "A quart of wheat for a denarius, and three quarts of barley for a denarius; and do not harm the oil and the wine."
>
> Revelation 6:5–6

The "third seal" is now opened, and a horseman comes forth who rides a "black" horse, holding a pair of scales. Amid the four creatures before God's throne, a voice cries out: "A quart of wheat for a denarius, and three quarts of barley for a denarius; and do not harm the oil and the wine." This horseman brings hunger and famine with him. Monetary systems worldwide will begin to fail, and inflation will skyrocket beyond anything the world economies have ever experienced. A quart of wheat, or three quarts of barley, is enough for only one person daily to sustain life, and a denarius is equivalent to one day's wages. People will have to work all day long to provide a day's food for themselves. "The oil and wine won't be harmed," indicating they will still be available, but the ordinary person cannot afford them. People won't be able to get enough food, so then chaos will ensue. Brother will hate brother, protesting and rioting will incur, and people will turn to looting, violence, and theft for basic supplies. Unprecedented anarchy and chaos will begin to fill the earth, and every nation will be affected.

> When He opened the fourth seal, I heard the voice of the fourth living creature saying, "Come and see." So I looked, and behold, a pale horse. And the name of him who sat on it was Death, and Hades followed with him. And power was given to them over a fourth of the earth, to kill with sword, with hunger, with death, and by the beasts of the earth.

> Revelation 6:7–8

Now, the "fourth seal" is opened. Its rider, Death, and Hades, following with him, appear on a pale horse. We are told that Death and Hades come to kill with the sword, with hunger, with pestilence, and by the beasts of the earth. The world's wild animals will resort to hunting and preying on humans in populated areas due to a lack of available food. Most people will be unbelievers by this point, although a few believers will survive the tribulation and enter the millennial kingdom. Those who die upon the opening of the fourth seal will not have Christ as their Redeemer. When they die, not only will they experience physical death, but their souls will immediately be in torment in Hades, awaiting the great white throne judgment. "Hades" is the place of temporary hell where unbelievers will await their final judgment before the lake of fire (Gehenna). All believers in Christ, however, immediately go into the presence of the Lord when they die by their faith in Christ. The believers who stay faithful to Christ or receive Him during tribulation become martyrs if killed. Their physical bodies will die, but their souls will be saved with Christ Jesus in heaven. The Greek word *Thanatos*, used here to describe the fourth horseman, can mean either death or pestilence. As bad as the COVID-19 epidemic has been worldwide, it is nothing compared to what will occur during the tribulation. The final horseman here will bring death to a fourth of the world's population, and because Hades follows Death, it will mean not only physical death but the second death of the soul. The world's population numbering between eight and nine billion will mean approximately two billion people will die on earth by the conclusion of the first four seals. God's wrath is being released and escalating with each seal.

During the tribulation, righteous people will still live on the earth. Many will find salvation in Christ during the tribulation. During the first half of the tribulation, there will be the "two witnesses" evangelizing around Jerusalem, much like God used the Old Testament prophets to proclaim His word through prophecy. Although no one was able to harm them beforehand, Satan, giving power to the antichrist, will be able to succeed in killing them by the midpoint of the tribulation. There also will be 144,000 celibate men coming from the twelve tribes of Israel (twelve thousand per tribe) who will be on the earth evangelizing for Christ. They will be sealed and protected by the Lord from His wrath. The 144,000 will minister in the second half of the tribulation. Near the end of the second half of the tribulation, an angel will evangelize to the people on earth in the heavens. So, you see, God shows His great love and mercy throughout the tribulation by allowing many to hear the gospel. Even during the outpouring of His wrath, God still wants many to be saved. Those who choose Christ as Savior during the tribulation, however, will most likely have to die in their faith. They will hold fast to their faith, refusing the "mark" of the antichrist even to the point of death, and thus, secure their eternal salvation. God cares more for your eternal soul rather than the death of your temporary physical body. Faith in Him assures us of receiving a new incorruptible body. He cares deeply for where you will spend your eternal days. Many will hear the gospel and come to Christ for salvation during the tribulation, but many will also have to die as martyrs at the hands of the "beast" and his government to save their souls. Some may die of hunger as martyrs because they refused the beast's mark. By not taking the mark of the beast, they won't be able to "buy or sell," so they won't be able to purchase food. Those who choose Christ over the mark of the beast will be unable to buy food or anything else, and they won't be able to sell anything to bring food to their families. They will be severely persecuted and forced to flee and hide from the beast, who is the antichrist. He and his military will hunt down the righteous who've refused his "mark." However, some will escape death at the hand of the antichrist and manage to find food enough to survive. We'll get into more of this when we reach chapters 13 and 14 of Revelation.

> When He opened the fifth seal, I saw under the altar the souls of those who had been slain for the word of God and for the testimony which they held. And they cried with a loud voice, saying, "How

long, O Lord, holy and true, until You judge and avenge our blood on those who dwell on the earth?" Then a white robe was given to each of them; and it was said to them that they should rest a little while longer, until both the number of their fellow servants and their brethren, who would be killed as they were, was completed.

Revelation 6:9–11

As we move on, Jesus continues and opens the "fifth seal." Here is revealed a plea for justice from the martyred saints of the tribulation. John sees the martyrs pleading for justice under the altar as they cry out to the Lord, "How long, O Lord, holy and true, until You judge and avenge our blood on those who dwell on the earth?" Regarding mankind's salvation, two truths will influence our eternal lives. We have a deadline for physical death, which is final. If one has not received Jesus Christ as Savior and Lord by the time their physical bodies die, it will be too late. There are no second chances. The other is the rapture. If you are alive and haven't given your life to Christ by the time of the rapture, you will be left behind, and you will have to experience the tribulation and undergo God's wrath on mankind and the earth. In verse 6:11, the martyred saints are given white robes and told by God to "rest a little while longer." He knows that more believers will be martyred in the tribulation because of their faith, so they must wait to be avenged "until both the number of their fellow servants and their brethren, who would be killed as they were, was completed." God knows these servants and their brethren will have to be martyred, but the eternal reward of their souls far outweighs the death of their physical bodies. Those who enter the tribulation who have not received Christ will find themselves in the worst of situations, such as never seen on the earth before. Not only will they be suffering the violence and depravity resulting from the plagues of the tribulation, but they will be hunted and executed because of their faith. It is much better to choose and receive Christ here and now before death, the rapture, or the onset of the tribulation rather than ignoring the truth and risking the eternal death of your soul. It is much more peaceful to come to Christ now than to do it during the tribulation, knowing you will have to be executed for your faith. No one becomes a martyr by dying of old age. Other than a handful of people who will survive and enter the millennial kingdom, most of those who come to Christ after the rapture must experience execution or die of starvation to hold onto their faith. These believers amid the tribulation are not part of the "church." They were still dead in their sins when the rapture event took place. These individuals are beloved by God, but they had not yet repented at the time of Jesus' appearance. Therefore, they were not part of the group of believers who were raptured before the start of the tribulation and considered as part of the "church." So, Jesus had not "gone and prepared a place for them," as was told to the disciples in John 14:1–4, which refers to the rapture event: Jesus said, "And if I go and prepare a place for you, I will come again and receive you to Myself; that where I am, there you may be also."

Nonetheless, God will still accept them into His family. These "saints" in heaven, described in Revelation 6:9–11, are separate from the raptured "church." They are the saints that have been martyred during the reign of the antichrist on earth.

Jesus now opens the "sixth seal":

> I looked when He opened the sixth seal, and be-
> hold, there was a great earthquake; and the sun
> became black as sackcloth of hair, and the moon
> became like blood. And the stars of heaven fell to
> the earth, as a fig tree drops its late figs when it is
> shaken by a mighty wind. Then the sky receded as a

scroll when it is rolled up, and every mountain and
island was moved out of its place.

Revelation 6:12–14

These events parallel those that will occur later in Revelation chapter 16 when the "sixth bowl" judgments are poured out but to a much greater degree. The bowl (or vial judgments, as the KJV refers to them) will be the most severe of all the prior judgments as God pours out His indignant wrath on the earth. Similarly, as the sixth seal is opened, verse 13 tells us that "the stars of heaven fell to the earth, as a fig tree drops its late figs when" a mighty wind shakes it. Then it says the "sky receded as a scroll when it is rolled up" and "every mountain and island was moved out of its place." When the sixth seal is opened, the heavens and the earth will shake, and meteors will hit the ground. These events suggest an actual change in the axis of the earth. A shift in the earth's axis could make the heavens appear to John like they have "receded as a scroll when it is rolled up," as the sky would look much different after these cataclysmic events occur. But regardless of how God chooses to bring these occurrences about, they will indeed happen according to His will. As the tribulation unfolds throughout the seven years, it will gradually increase in severity as judgments are unleashed. Our life here in today's modern world, as chaotic as it seems, will be like a walk in the park compared to what will occur during the tribulation, beginning with the opening of the seven seals. Some claim that the seven seals are opened at the midpoint of the tribulation, but this belief is false. The first seal brings the antichrist with his deceitful covenant of peace in hand for Israel, which must occur at the onset of the seven-year tribulation. This will be a deceptively false covenant of peace between Israel and the antichrist because, at the midpoint of the tribulation, he will fail to honor the agreement he had made with them. The building of the temple will be finished during the first three-and-a-half years, then the "beast" at the midpoint of the tribulation will stand in the temple and proclaim himself as "God." At that time, the beast will take claim of the temple and set up his "image" to be worshipped.

There are those today who think they can continue to reject Christ, enjoy their worldly lifestyles, and have plenty of time during the tribulation to choose God should they decide. But these people don't realize the severe suffering they will endure, so they presume they can "take their chances" and bide their time. But during the tribulation, many people will become hard-hearted and choose to believe the lie instead of the truth. Today is the day of salvation. If you think you'll have plenty of time to come to Christ, think soberly, for no one knows the day or hour that Christ will appear. The great tribulation will be a dreadful and horrifying time of God's wrath, and no one should take the ramifications of it lightly.

> And the kings of the earth, the great men, the rich men, the commanders, the mighty men, every slave and every free man, hid themselves in the caves and in the rocks of the mountains, and said to the mountains and rocks, "Fall on us and hide us from the face of Him who sits on the throne and from the wrath of the Lamb! For the great day of His wrath has come, and who is able to stand?"

Revelation 6:15–17

As the sixth seal is opened, the earth will be experiencing large-scale cataclysmic events that no man has ever witnessed. Everyone will be in a state of panic and terror because it will seem like the end of the world has come. Men will want to seek shelter and hide, hoping the rocks and mountains will fall on them and kill them swiftly rather than endure the fury of God's wrath. Realizing that God has come in His wrath to punish them all will strike fear. In these final passages of

Revelation chapter 6, note that this time is called "the great day of His wrath" and "the wrath of the Lamb." Clearly, this shows that God's wrath has been pouring out well before the second half of the tribulation. In Revelation chapter 7, verse 14, we find the only mention of the term "great tribulation" in the entire book of Revelation, and it does not explicitly refer to the last three-and-a-half years of the seventieth week. Those who hold onto a "mid-tribulation rapture theory" completely ignore verses 6:17 and 7:14. They assert that there is no wrath until the second half of the tribulation and that the "seventh trumpet" judgment marks the beginning of the second half. They see it as the "trumpet of God" and "the last trumpet" that hails at the onset of the rapture, as detailed in 1 Thessalonians 4:16 and 1 Corinthians 15:52. But this is inaccurate, according to Scripture. A proper conclusion would be that the entire tribulation is the outpouring of God's wrath for the reasons I've stated earlier, based on the trauma that plagues the earth and humanity, including large-scale deaths due to the wrath that is released upon the world when the seven seals are opening. The "great day of His wrath," therefore, begins at the onset of the seven-year tribulation when the antichrist makes a false covenant of peace with Israel. After the opening of the first six seals, a quarter of the world's population has been killed, and those who remain suffer greatly from famine, pestilence, and the plagues of the seals. However, it will worsen when we move on to the trumpet judgments. The "seals" and the "trumpet" judgments are chastisements to the people on earth to bring them to "repentance," but they are extremely harsher than the chastisements used by the spirit of God today to help a Christian grow in their walk with Jesus Christ. These are severe chastisements that cause death to a quarter of the world's population. We are also told in 1 Thessalonians 5:9 that God has not appointed us to wrath, and Romans 5:9 states, "Much more then, having now been justified by His blood, we shall be saved from wrath through Him." Jesus Himself assures us, in Revelation 3:10, "I also will keep you from the hour of trial which shall come upon the whole world." The church cannot be on earth during the day of His wrath because God's promises are true. We are kept from the hour of trial in Christ Jesus. By this time on the tribulation timeline, the church has already been "caught up" and translated or risen to meet Jesus in the air before God's wrath. I must conclude that the scriptural truth of the rapture is that it occurs at the end of the church age when the fullness of the Gentiles has come in, just before the lawless one appears after the Lamb opens the first seal.

> After these things I saw four angels standing at the four corners of the earth, holding the four winds of the earth, that the wind should not blow on the earth, on the sea, or on any tree. Then I saw another angel ascending from the east, having the seal of the living God. And he cried with a loud voice to the four angels to whom it was granted to harm the earth and the sea, saying, "Do not harm the earth, the sea, or the trees till we have sealed the servants of our God on their foreheads." And I heard the number of those who were sealed. One hundred and forty-four thousand of all the tribes of the children of Israel were sealed.

Revelation 7:1–4

Chapter 7 of Revelation is an interlude from the judgments and speaks of the 144,000 and four angels holding back the winds. The 144,000 are servants of God who are evangelizing during the tribulation. There are twelve thousand messianic and celibate Jews from each tribe of Israel, adding up to 144,000, as I mentioned previously. The tribe of Dan is not here because of their commitment to idolatry, so they are twelve tribes. Four angels from the four corners of the earth hold back the winds until the servants of God are sealed on their foreheads. God's love always ensures His own people's safety before unleashing any wrath onto the world. When they are released, these winds will affect the weather severely, producing drought and severe hardship upon the earth. Theologian Matthew Henry also compares these winds held back as "errors and corruption in religion," "doing much hurt to the church" by which those "who are unstable are shaken and carried to and fro" (also see Ephesians 4:14, KJV). He writes,

> Here we have an account of the restraint laid upon the winds. By these winds, we suppose, are meant those errors and corruptions in religion which would occasion a great deal of trouble and mischief to the church of God. Sometimes the Holy Spirit is compared to the wind: here the spirits of error are compared to the four winds, contrary one to another, but doing much hurt to the church, the garden and vineyard of God, breaking the branches and blasting the fruits of his plantation. The devil is called the prince of the power of the air; he, by a great wind, overthrew the house of Job's eldest son. Errors are as wind, by which those who are unstable are shaken, and carried to and fro, they are restrained by the ministry of angels, standing on the four corners of the earth, intimating that the spirit of error cannot go forth till God permits it, and that the angels minister to the good of the church by restraining its enemies. Their restraint was only for a season, and that was till the servants of God were sealed in their foreheads. God has a particular care and concern for his own servants in times of temptation and corruption, and he has a way to

secure them from the common infection; he first establishes them, and then he tries them; he has the timing of their trials in his own hand. An account of the sealing of the servants of God, where observe, to whom this work was committed—to an angel, another angel. While some of the angels were employed to restrain Satan and his agents, another angel was employed to mark out and distinguish the faithful servants of God. How they were distinguished—the seal of God was set upon their foreheads, a seal known to him, and as plain as if it appeared in their foreheads; by this mark they were set apart for mercy and safety in the worst of times.

As the Holy Spirit is often compared to wind, so is Satan, the prince of the air with his forces. As these four winds are being held back, Matthew Henry identifies these winds as Satan's forces going out against the good of the church. Angels are the restraining force here, doing God's will to restrain the winds until the servants of God are sealed on their foreheads by yet another angel.

After these things I looked, and behold, a great multitude which no one could number, of all nations, tribes, peoples, and tongues, standing before the throne and before the Lamb, clothed with white robes, with palm branches in their hands, and crying out with a loud voice, saying, "Salvation belongs to our God who sits on the throne, and to the Lamb!" All the angels stood around the throne and the elders and the four living creatures, and fell on their faces before the throne and worshiped God, saying:

"Amen! Blessing and glory and wisdom,

Thanksgiving and honor and power and might, Be to our God forever and ever. Amen."

Then one of the elders answered, saying to me, "Who are these arrayed in white robes, and where did they come from?"

And I said to him, "Sir, you know."

So he said to me, "These are the ones who come out of the great tribulation, and washed their robes and made them white in the blood of the Lamb. Therefore they are before the throne of God, and serve Him day and night in His temple. And He who sits on the throne will dwell among them. They shall neither hunger anymore nor thirst anymore; the sun shall not strike them, nor any heat; for the Lamb who is in the midst of the throne will shepherd them and lead them to living fountains of waters. And God will wipe away every tear from their eyes."

Revelation 7:9–17

All the angels, elders, and the four living creatures stood around the throne "and fell on their faces before the throne and worshiped God, saying: 'Amen! Blessing and glory and wisdom, Thanksgiving and honor and power and might be to our God forever and ever. Amen.'"

We see many people in white robes, "of all nations, tribes, peoples, and tongues, standing before the throne and before the Lamb," waving palm branches, symbolizing purity and victory. These are the saints of the tribulation, those martyred, who are complete in number now and with the Lord in the heavenly realm. They ran a good race and finished the course.

They wear white robes, denoting their priesthood and purity, and they come from all nations and peoples of the earth, suggesting to us that in heaven, we will be individuals of many ethnicities, uniquely alike but diverse in our unique differences, all of one body of saints. Like a loving parent, the Lamb will comfort His children, those who have endured such hardship and persevered, and He will wipe away their tears.

Now we move beyond the interlude of chapter 7 to chapter 8 of Revelation, as we conclude the seal judgments, and the "seventh seal" is opened.

> When He opened the seventh seal, there was silence in heaven for about half an hour. And I saw the seven angels who stand before God, and to them were given seven trumpets. Then another angel, having a golden censer, came and stood at the altar. He was given much incense, that he should offer it with the prayers of all the saints upon the golden altar which was before the throne. And the smoke of the incense, with the prayers of the saints, ascended before God from the angel's hand. Then the angel took the censer, filled it with fire from the altar, and threw it to the earth. And there were noises, thunderings, lightnings, and an earthquake.
>
> So the seven angels who had the seven trumpets prepared themselves to sound.
>
> Revelation 8:1–6

Upon the opening of the seventh seal, we see a pause of silence in heaven for half an hour. The seven angels before the throne are given seven trumpets; the trumpet judgments are now imminent. Another angel stood before the altar with a golden censer containing incense (the saints' prayers) that ascended before God from his hand. These could be the prayers of the martyred saints or the prayers given of all the saints throughout the church age; we do not know for sure. The angel then fills the "golden censer" with fire and casts it down to the earth, bringing "noises, thunderings, lightnings, and an earthquake." Then, the angels with trumpets prepared themselves to sound.

CHAPTER 2

THE SEVEN ANGELS AND THEIR TRUMPETS

The "Trumpet" Judgments

One of the purposes of the "trumpet judgments" and the "bowl judgments" is to cleanse the earth from the results of sin and to be a part of the redemption process. The "trumpet judgments" resemble the plagues of Egypt. They have a three-fold purpose, similar to Egypt's plagues in the book of Exodus. These plagues here will:

1. Prove the sovereign power and presence of God.

2. Show how powerless science is, which has become a god to man.

3. Show mankind that Satan cannot win.

The first angel sounds his trumpet, and hail and fire mingled with blood is cast upon the earth. One-third of the world's trees and all of its grass are burned. This drought may have been caused by the lack of rain during the "seal judgments" when the angels held back the winds of the earth. This event would cause standard weather patterns to shift, leading to severe drought and dry vegetation. The planet would be vulnerable to forest fires sweeping across and burning up a third of the earth. Hailstones will be gigantic, unlike any hail we know of today, and fear and confusion will escalate among the earth's inhabitants.

"Then the second angel sounded: And something like a great mountain burning with fire was thrown into the sea, and a third of the sea became blood. And a third of the living creatures in the sea died, and a third of the ships were destroyed" (Revelation 8:8–9).

This sounds very much like a giant asteroid. The asteroid would have caused such an impact that a tsunami or tidal wave destroyed one-third of the sea creatures and one-third of the world's ships, turning one-third of the oceans into blood. If an asteroid were to explode on impact, it could also create a large amount of dust, perhaps red dust, that would turn the sea red, similar to the red tides that occur and kill fish in our time. Or it could mean actual blood. In the second trumpet judgment, one-third of the oceans turn to blood. But when we arrive at the parallel second bowl judgment, "The entire ocean" will turn to blood, not just one-third. A fiery mass, much like a mountain (possibly more enormous), would not naturally change water into blood, nor would it destroy a third of the world's ships. Still, these events will occur as written by God's power in the trumpet judgments. The book of Revelation is Jesus' revealing to man what would occur in the end times. If God said it would happen, it certainly will.

> Then the third angel sounded: And a great star fell from heaven, burning like a torch, and it fell on a third of the rivers and on the springs of water. The name of the star is Wormwood. A third of the waters became wormwood, and many men died from the water, because it was made bitter.
>
> Revelation 8:10–11

This star was most likely a meteor that turned the waters

bitter. This meteor is called "Wormwood" because the water turned poisonous and killed many people. "Wormwood" refers to the dark green oil produced by the plant of the same name, which people used to kill intestinal worms in the past. In Amos 6:12, the Hebrew word used in the verse can also refer to "hemlock" (in the RSV, "wormwood"), a bitter poisonous substance. In either case, the waters will become toxic to mankind, and men will not be able to drink it.

"Then the fourth angel sounded: And a third of the sun was struck, a third of the moon, and a third of the stars, so that a third of them were darkened. A third of the day did not shine, and likewise the night" (Revelation 8:12).

Here, God strikes the heavenly bodies with a plague, causing the sun, moon, and stars only to give out a third of their light. This dimmer luminescence will significantly affect the light of day and night, bringing darkness upon the earth. The lightness of the day will be lessened by a third, and the darkness of the night diminished by a third. The sun, moon, and stars will be much dimmer than we're currently used to experiencing on earth. It will bring a dreadful darkness upon the earth that causes even more depression and anxiety in the hearts of humanity. It will cause continual hopelessness in those who remain in the world.

"And I looked, and I heard an angel flying through the midst of heaven, saying with a loud voice, 'Woe, woe, woe to the inhabitants of the earth, because of the remaining blasts of the trumpet of the three angels who are about to sound!'" (Revelation 8:13).

The first four trumpets were directed at nature (although people's lives will be affected by them). In comparison, the last three trumpets are aimed at people. Also, the last three trumpets are known as the three "woes" because of the warning from the angel, "Woe, woe, woe to the inhabitants of the earth." The fifth trumpet is the first of the three "woes." Whenever the word "woe" is used in Scripture, it denotes a severe and dire judgment from God. The fifth and sixth trumpets will be the last chance for people to repent on the earth.

> Then the fifth angel sounded: And I saw a star fallen from heaven to the earth. To him was given the key to the bottomless pit. And he opened the bottomless pit, and smoke arose out of the pit like the smoke of a great furnace. So the sun and the air were darkened because of the smoke of the pit. Then out of the smoke locusts came upon the earth. And to them was given power, as the scorpions of the earth have power.
>
> Revelation 9:1–3

When the "fifth trumpet" sounds, we are told of a star descending from heaven. The "star" is the fallen angel Satan, who is given the key to "the bottomless pit." The Greek word *abussos* is used here, which means "abyss" or "bottomless pit." The Jews believed, and Scripture confirms, that Sheol (Hebrew) or Hades (Greek) had three unique compartments. (1) "Tartarus" is a special place for the angels that had "left their first estate" (heaven) before the flood occurred when God started over with Noah and his family. These are the angels that took human women and produced the half-breed Nephilim (or giants), who were half-human and half-angelic beings that were on the earth before the flood. Tartarus is also known as the "abyss" or "bottomless pit," where certain other demonic spirits are confined and where Satan will be bound for a thousand years at the beginning of the millennial reign. (2) "Hades/Sheol," which is sometimes referred to as a temporary hell, is a place of torment where the unrighteous await their trial at the great white throne judgment, and (3) "The bosom of Abraham," a paradise where all those deemed righteous in the Old Testament awaited their Messiah (Christ). "The bosom of Abraham" is empty today because when Jesus died and descended, He proclaimed who He was to them, and they believed. He released these righteous souls to be with Him from then on and took them to heaven, awaiting the redemption of their bodies. Now, in our present era of the church age, following Jesus' death, burial, and resurrection, the souls of saved believers in Christ go into His presence immediately upon death to await the redemption of their bodies. As believers, awake or asleep, the redemption of our bodies will happen when the rapture/resurrection takes place. "Then out of the smoke locusts came upon the earth. And to them was given power, as the scorpions of the earth have power." In chapter 9, verse 3, the locusts are revealed to be demonic creatures emerging from the smoke. They are scorpion-like creatures with powerful stings to torment those who worship the beast:

> They were commanded not to harm the grass of the earth, or any green thing, or any tree, but only those men who do not have the seal of God on their foreheads. And they were not given authority to kill them, but to torment them for five months. Their torment was like the torment of a scorpion when it strikes a man. In those days men will seek death and will not find it; they will desire to die, and death will flee from them.

> The shape of the locusts was like horses prepared for battle. On their heads were crowns of something like gold, and their faces were like the faces of men. They had hair like women's hair, and their teeth were like lions' teeth. And they had breastplates like breastplates of iron, and the sound

of their wings was like the sound of chariots with many horses running into battle. They had tails like scorpions, and there were stings in their tails. Their power was to hurt men five months. And they had as king over them the angel of the bottomless pit, whose name in Hebrew is Abaddon, but in Greek he has the name Apollyon.

Revelation 9:4–11

We are given a vivid description in the Scripture of demonic locusts that emerge from the smoke to torment the wicked. The wicked upon the earth will be plagued by these demon locusts for five months by these agonizing tormentors, unable to escape from them. Those on the earth who are righteous in Christ and have been sealed by God's mark on their foreheads (the 144,000 and those who come to Christ during the tribulation) will not be tormented by these demons. However, none of us who have faith in Christ now will be there to experience these locusts or any of the judgment plagues. Remember, the church at this time will already have been raptured and translated or resurrected and will be in heaven with Jesus. We are told in these verses that people will suffer so intensely that they will want to die, but they won't be able to. The locust's sting will be so severe and excruciating that people will want to kill themselves. They will try but fail, "as death will flee from them." In their futile efforts to escape their torment, these people will not die; God will not allow it until the five months have ended. Death is a blessing to the child of God, but for the wicked unbeliever, it is the beginning of eternal torment. The suffering from these locusts is a taste of what will come for these plagued people. If they refuse to repent, they will be judged and cast into the lake of fire, following their judgment at the great white throne, and suffer for all eternity for their sins simply because they had disregarded God's gift of salvation. Instead, they refused to accept Christ as their only opportunity for salvation. All our souls are eternal regardless of where we spend eternity; it's just a matter of location, and in the second resurrection (the resurrection of condemnation) at the end of the tribulation and before the millennial kingdom, the wicked will be resurrected and given imperishable bodies just before those without Christ will be judged. At "the great white throne judgment," they will stand trial before God. They'll be cast into the lake of burning sulfur, unable to end their torment in the fire, where they will endure endless suffering. This event is known as the "second death" in the Scriptures. Those without Christ to pay for their sins will be cast into hell (Gehenna, the burning lake), and they won't be able to escape the consequences. Like those on earth who try to flee from the locusts through death, they can't end their torment. In verse 7, we see the faces of the locusts are like the faces of men, and this characteristic implies these creatures have cunning and intelligence. Then we are told, "And they had as king over them the angel of the bottomless pit, whose name in Hebrew is Abaddon, but in Greek he has the name Apollyon." The Hebrew name "Abaddon" ("Apollyon" in Greek) means "destruction" or "destroyer." Here, we have another name for Satan, the "king" of the demonic locusts unleashed from the bottomless pit.

> One woe is past. Behold, still two more woes are coming after these things.

> Then the sixth angel sounded: And I heard a voice from the four horns of the golden altar which is before God, saying to the sixth angel who had the trumpet, "Release the four angels who are bound at the great river Euphrates." So the four angels, who had been prepared for the hour and day and month and year, were released to kill a third of mankind.

> Revelation 9:12–15

When the "sixth trumpet" sounds, four angelic beings come forth by the angel who sounded the trumpet. These are satanic angels, fallen creatures whom God has kept bound and incarcerated since the beginning of man's existence. They have been held back for this hour, released from the river Euphrates to accomplish their mission. These fallen angels were so fierce that God had to keep them bound for six thousand years. God is releasing them "who had been prepared for the hour and day and month and year," and as a result, a third of humanity will be slaughtered. During the first four "seal judgments," when the four horses of the apocalypse were released, a quarter of the world's population was destroyed, and now another third of humankind is destroyed by these fallen angels.

CHAPTER 3

INTERLUDE:
A DEMONIC ARMY

Now the number of the army of the horsemen was two hundred million; I heard the number of them. And thus I saw the horses in the vision: those who sat on them had breastplates of fiery red, hyacinth blue, and sulfur yellow; and the heads of the horses were like the heads of lions; and out of their mouths came fire, smoke, and brimstone. By these three plagues a third of mankind was killed—by the fire and the smoke and the brimstone which came out of their mouths. For their power is in their mouth and in their tails; for their tails are like serpents, having heads; and with them they do harm.

But the rest of mankind, who were not killed by these plagues, did not repent of the works of their hands, that they should not worship demons, and idols of gold, silver, brass, stone, and wood, which can neither see nor hear nor walk. And they did not repent of their murders or their sorceries or their sexual immorality or their thefts.

Revelation 9:16–21

The description of these two million horsemen paints a

grotesque and horrific visual of a vast army. Whether they are men or demonic can only be determined by whether we can take these passages literally or figuratively. Throughout history, no other army of men on earth has equaled these numbers in the past. It is more solid to conclude this is a supernaturally conceived army of demonic forces similar to what we saw in the demonic locusts. With God, anything is possible, no matter how astounding it may seem. The events of the tribulation will be events that man has never seen before, some fantastic. However, through all of these things, including the grand scale of deaths that will occur in such a short time, men will still not repent. Those who survive these plagues will have hardened hearts and cling to their sin despite witnessing and experiencing the suffering that is happening to and around them. Few will repent. They will think it foolish to be martyred for the sake of their souls, and many will reject the Lord their God during this unprecedented time of trouble.

Throughout the history of humanity, there have been people who reject God and many who have received God through the Lord and Savior, Jesus Christ. Paul said it is the goodness of God that brings a man to repentance (Romans 2:4). God wants everyone to repent and turn away from the world's sins and follow Him. Repentance is just a "change of mind" to turn away from the world and to God. God is always good, even when He has to do what is just and proper. He must always punish the disobedient to stay true to His Word. The Scriptures provide prophetic images of the "end times," which detail God's coming wrath and the judgments that will come upon the earth and all who dwell on it. But man hardens his heart against these judgments of God.

Humanity, by their pride and rebellion, rejects the notion that any of these things could be true. But just as 87 percent of the biblical prophecies given by God have come true already, with not one failing, so will all the predictions of God come true in their proper time. The judgments of God won't bring men to repentance, but the goodness of God will. One of the works of the Holy Spirit is to draw men to Christ for salvation. God wants us to know the prophetic events that will occur one day so we can keep watch for them and know He is God. The Almighty God wants us to seek Him out and come to know Him through the Son, Jesus Christ. I encourage everyone to seek God through Christ and develop a good relationship. Through His Word, as written in the Scriptures and by the Holy Spirit given to all who believe in Christ, you will come to know the goodness of God. It starts by trusting and believing in Christ as your Lord and Savior. He is righteous and good, and He loves us all! He doesn't want to lose anyone because of sin, and His goodness and amazing grace are made evident by the gift of His only Son, who is the Lord Jesus Christ! He is the goodness of God who became flesh, and He is the only way to reconcile us back to God.

The "judgments" reveal that God is a God of justice and must deal with sin; however, He is long-suffering and patient toward His creation so that He may save many. Evil must be eradicated through judgment because it separates us from our Creator God. God must continuously work on separating us from sin so we are not separated from Him. He who dwells within us is mightier than he who lives in the world. We were created to be with God. We are lost without God. It was never intended for us to go through life without Him. Satan, throughout the church age, has tried to show us otherwise because, without God, we are dead in our sins. Throughout history, the devil has deceived humanity through lies and deception, and he continues to do so today. Satan is the father of lies and a murderer from the beginning (John 8:44). For God to make everything right again, He had to send His only Son to save all who would hear the truth. Jesus will return and deal with the wicked on this earth, and He will restore the earth and establish His kingdom. During the millennial reign of Christ, earth will become a much better place. However, at the end of the thousand years, mortal men will be enticed by the adversary and will revolt. Satan will lead them to attack the Lord and His saints in Jerusalem. God will destroy them with fire from heaven, and following that, He will judge those who died without Christ as their Savior and abolish all sin. He will create a new heaven and restore the earth where God's people will live eternally with Him, and no evil will exist. God's wrath has to be poured out on the world to end all sin that separates us from Him. As Christians, we must talk about God's judgments from time to time as written, but we must concentrate on His goodness. It is here that salvation will be found in Christ Jesus. As we continue, the seventh trumpet is about to sound, and it will usher in the bowl judgments. But first, our Lord has revealed some other things to us.

At this point, six trumpet judgments have occurred, bringing catastrophes upon the earth. Now, as we progress through the revealing, we have another "interlude" as we break from the trumpet judgments. Before the seventh trumpet sounds, John describes a vision of another future event: the second coming of Christ to claim the earth and begin His reign. This magnificent angel gives us a little insight into the second coming of the Lord with a declaration that it will soon take place. We are told, in Psalm 24:1, "The earth is the LORD's, and all its fullness, The world and those who dwell therein," and in Psalm chapter 2, we see, "Ask of Me, and I will give You The nations for Your inheritance, And the ends of the earth for Your possession." So, here in Revelation, we have the prophetic vision of a mighty angel who, by the power of the Almighty God, declares how and when "the mystery of God would be finished" (Revelation 10:7). It is a foretelling of when Jesus comes again to possess what He purchased by His blood.

"I saw still another mighty angel coming down from heaven, clothed with a cloud. And a rainbow was on his head, his face was like the sun, and his feet like pillars of fire" (Revelation 10:1).

As we begin chapter 10 of Revelation, John is given a vision of a messenger, an angel whose description is similar to that of Jesus Christ. He sees the angel "clothed with a cloud" and a rainbow upon his head. This parallels the Lord's description in Revelation 1:7, which describes Him coming with the clouds: "Behold, He is coming with clouds, and every eye will see Him, even they who pierced Him. And all the tribes of the earth will mourn because of Him. Even so, Amen." The rainbow was the covenant of God, and a rainbow surrounds the throne of God, but here it surrounds the angel's head.

Not only is the rainbow a reminder of God's promise to man, but it is also a natural result when the sun shines through a cloud. So here in chapter 10, we see similarities to John's description of Jesus in chapter 1, which shows this angel messenger to be in the likeness of Christ. Many have identified this mighty angel as Jesus Himself because some of the imagery also applies to Him. Revelation 1:15–16 also describes Jesus with His countenance, "like the sun shining in its strength." However, this angelic being is not Jesus Himself. This angel is not divine; he is a servant of God. Angels are never clearly identified with Jesus in the book of Revelation or the New Testament. However, Jesus is recognized as the "angel of the Lord" in the Old Testament. A better identification of similarities would be with the archangel known as Michael. However, he is not Michael the archangel since it doesn't name him here like other passages. There are similarities between this mighty angel and the archangel Michael as he is described in Daniel 12:1, which does refer to him by name:

> At that time Michael shall stand up, The great prince
> who stands watch over the sons of your people; And

there shall be a time of trouble, Such as never was since there was a nation, Even to that time. And at that time your people shall be delivered, Every one who is found written in the book.

We know this is a different angel than Michael. We also know it is not Christ because this angel sets his feet on the earth. Jesus won't step upon the earth again until the second coming, before the end of the tribulation.

"He had a little book open in his hand. And he set his right foot on the sea and his left foot on the land" (Revelation 10:2).

In Revelation chapter 5, we saw the scroll with seven seals in heaven. John was told no man was worthy to take the scroll or loose the seals. We find that it was the title deed to the earth. Once the Lamb began opening the seven seals, the scroll, or book, is now open. Many believe that this towering angel holding an "open" book in his hand holds the book of the seven seals, representing the authority and the right to the earth that Jesus had obtained by sacrificing His life. But John used different words to describe the scroll of Revelation 5:1 and the little book written about here. It is best to see them as different yet closely related. Some even think it is likely to be the scroll eaten by Ezekiel in Ezekiel 2:9 and 3:3. We honestly don't know for certainty, as the Scripture doesn't tell us.

John sees the angel with one foot on the land and one foot on the sea, conveying the image of possession, which is what Jesus is about to do with the earth. When Jesus went to the cross, He paid the price for redemption. By His sacrifice on the cross, the Lord redeemed the world back to Himself. It was initially His; He had intended dominion to belong to man, but when man fell into sin (Adam and Eve), Adam handed dominion over to Satan due to disobedience. Jesus called Satan "the prince of this world" (John 14:30, KJV). Paul called him "the god of this age" and "the prince of the power of the air" (2 Corinthians 4:4, Ephesians 2:2). Satan tempted Jesus by offering Him the world if He would only bow down and worship him. Still, Jesus came to redeem the world, paying the price for it with His life and shedding His blood. He would not be tempted to deviate from His mission. The precious blood of Jesus Christ saves us, but He has not taken possession of what He has purchased yet. Paul tells us, in Romans 8, "Not only that, but we also who have the firstfruits of the Spirit, even we ourselves groan within ourselves, eagerly waiting for the adoption, the redemption of our body" (Romans 8:23). So, our "redemption" still needs to be made complete. Paul also told us, in Ephesians 1:13–14,

> In Him you also trusted, after you heard the word of truth, the gospel of your salvation; in whom also, having believed, you were sealed with the Holy Spirit of promise, who is the guarantee of our inheritance until the redemption of the purchased possession, to the praise of His glory.

Jesus taught about two resurrections: the "resurrection of life" and "the resurrection of condemnation." However, the resurrection of life (first resurrection) consists of "two parts" and takes place at two different times. There is a resurrection before the beginning of the tribulation (rapture) and a resurrection at the end of the tribulation, just before the millennium. The second part of the first resurrection is for those who died in Christ during the tribulation. These will be resurrected and joined in heaven with the saints who were raptured before the beginning of the tribulation. The resurrection of condemnation (second resurrection) will occur just before the great white throne judgment (immediately after Satan is cast into the lake of fire, following the millennium).

Here, the condemned will be judged on their own merits

without having the Penal Substitute of Christ Jesus as their saving Redeemer, and they'll be cast into the lake of fire for their sins. In Hebrews 2:8, we are told that God has put all things in subjection under Him, but we do not yet see all things in subjection. The world is still in rebellion against Him. The world has yet to be brought into His power under His reign. We know that God has put everything under Him, but we don't yet see them manifest. We see Jesus, who was made a little lower than the angels for the suffering of death, crowned with glory and honor. So, as Paul told us, we and all creation groan together, waiting, travailing for that glorious day when the Lord will come and claim that which He purchased. When He takes possession of that which already belongs to Him. We, as Christians, rejoice in the Holy Spirit and the power of the Spirit in our lives, which sustains and keeps us until He comes back to receive His church. So, we are anxiously awaiting full redemption for God's creation and for the Lord to reign in heaven and on earth. For this reason, Jesus told us to pray, "Your kingdom come. Your will be done On earth as it is in heaven" (Luke 11:2).

> And cried with a loud voice, as when a lion roars. When he cried out, seven thunders uttered their voices. Now when the seven thunders uttered their voices, I was about to write; but I heard a voice from heaven saying to me, "Seal up the things which the seven thunders uttered, and do not write them."

> Revelation 10:3–4

The angel messenger now cries out with a roar like a lion and gets the attention of the seven thunders. We're unaware of who these seven thunders are, but they are most likely angels with a unique message. The cry of the mighty angel will shake open the mouths of the seven thunders, and they will begin talking. However, John is instructed by a voice from heaven not to write them down. We can only speculate as to what these thunders proclaimed. God only gives us the things He wants us to know. Some secrets are revealed to us by God, and others are not. We can assume that we don't need to know, or God would have told us.

> The angel whom I saw standing on the sea and on the land raised up his hand to heaven and swore by Him who lives forever and ever, who created heaven and the things that are in it, the earth and the things that are in it, and the sea and the things that are in it, that there should be delay no longer, but in the days of the sounding of the seventh angel, when he is about to sound, the mystery of God would be finished, as He declared to His servants the prophets.

> Revelation 10:5–7

At this point, all on earth will not doubt that this tribulation results from God's handiwork. They will realize that a Grand Creator completely controlled the created earth they worshipped over God. What was taking place throughout all the nations of the earth, the deaths and cataclysmic destruction, was happening exactly how God said it would. It would happen to all those who turned their backs on Him in rebellion. This prophecy, written thousands of years ago, is now being fulfilled. The angel took a solemn oath on God the Creator and all things He created that this was all true. When the seventh angel blows his trumpet, it will lead to the "mystery of God" concluding. In this context, the mystery of God probably refers to the unfolding of His resolution of all things and the finishing of His plan of the ages. A mystery of God is a truth revealed at a certain point. The mystery here may refer to the "millennial reign of Christ" we are told about in Revelation chapter 20. Prophets, including Isaiah, Daniel, Jeremiah, and Zechariah, as well as some others, were given a glimpse of the coming one-thousand-year reign of Christ on earth as foretold in their prophecies. Now, Satan's dominion over the earth is about to come to an end. The Messiah (the Christ) will take His proper place on His earthly throne as Lord and King. Now, the mystery will be seen in its whole reality.

> Then the voice which I heard from heaven spoke to me again and said, "Go, take the little book which is open in the hand of the angel who stands on the sea and on the earth."
>
> So I went to the angel and said to him, "Give me the little book."
>
> And he said to me, "Take and eat it; and it will make your stomach bitter, but it will be as sweet as honey in your mouth."
>
> Then I took the little book out of the angel's hand and ate it, and it was as sweet as honey in my mouth. But when I had eaten it, my stomach became bitter. And he said to me, "You must prophesy again about many peoples, nations, tongues, and kings."
>
> Revelation 10:8–11

In Psalm 119:103, we find a description of one of the excellencies of the "Word of God," which reads, "How sweet are Your words to my taste, Sweeter than honey to my mouth!" Ezekiel also ate a scroll and thought it was as sweet as honey. God's Word is good, nourishing, and refreshing to the soul, sweet as honey. When reading future prophecies, the messages can sometimes be unpleasant. Revelation 10:9–10 shows that God's Word can be bittersweet. John was told to eat the little book, devouring the Word of God, as we sometimes "devour" a good book that we can't seem to put down. The Word was sweet because it signified that God's plan was in motion to make all things new again. This would put an end to sin and the wickedness of the fallen world and avenge the righteous who have suffered at the hands of the wicked. The reality of God's Word and plan in motion would soon come to fruition. Still, it was also bitter that those with "hardened hearts," who were many, would have to perish to accomplish His purpose. The earth would be put through disasters and convulsions. God condemns no one; they condemn themselves by rejecting God's gift of salvation and forgiveness, Jesus Christ. God is a righteous and just God, and He always does what is right and good, but it can be bitter for the righteous in Christ to witness the peril and destruction of those we love around us. It's difficult to imagine the catastrophic events that unfold when the seals are broken and the judgments are poured out upon the world. As believers, we find comfort in the thought of the coming kingdom and our Lord's reign on earth. Yet it is bittersweet because we know many will remain lost.

> Then I was given a reed like a measuring rod. And the angel stood, saying, "Rise and measure the temple of God, the altar, and those who worship there. But leave out the court which is outside the temple, and do not measure it, for it has been given to the Gentiles. And they will tread the holy city underfoot for forty-two months."

> Revelation 11:1–2

The scripture above tells us that the temple is to be rebuilt because this is yet a future event. There has been no temple since Jesus went to the cross, even in our present age, for Christ brought in the new covenant, and God now resides in believers' hearts, not in a "temple." Christians get excited when they see efforts to rebuild the temple in Israel; however, we should understand that the motivation behind rebuilding the temple is not of God at all. Their desire to have a place of sacrifice for sin is a denial of Jesus Christ, who atoned for all sin when He died on the cross. Christians believe that all sacrifice for sin was finished at the cross, and any other sacrifice for sin is an offense to God because it denies the completed work of Christ. The temple rebuilding is an event that takes place during the tribulation period after the church has been raptured. As I explained in the prologue to this book, the antichrist will be revealed before the tribulation begins. Russia, Turkey, Iran, Sudan, Libya, and others will gather to invade Israel just before the seventieth week of Daniel (Ezekiel 38–39). Before any great harm can be inflicted upon Israel, God will intervene and destroy those who attempt to do so. Once the antichrist (lawless one) is revealed, he will soon after make a peaceful covenant with Israel, and part of the covenant would be that they could rebuild the temple of God along with performing animal sacrifices. It would take a "man of peace" to accomplish this, a man like the antichrist who will win the hearts of the world as their savior, even the Jews, with his remarkable political skills, which he will use to restore their temple on the "temple mount." With its immense bloodshed, the Ezekiel war will "open the door" for the antichrist to appear on the world stage, masquerading as a "man of peace."

Even now, in our present time, there is a group of Jewish priests making plans and manufacturing the articles of the temple, along with the priestly attire that the sacrificial priests will be wearing. There is a school where rabbis teach young men how to perform animal sacrifices according to Levitical law. They are getting ready for a new temple to be built, but it doesn't happen until the church has been taken out and the "lawless one" has arrived on the scene. In Revelation 11:2

above, we were told that the Gentiles would trample the outer courts of the temple and the city for forty-two months, which is three-and-a-half-years, and this probably occurs after the midpoint, during the last half of the seven-year tribulation also referred to as the "great tribulation." There is an assumption that the Dome of the Rock shrine stands in the place of the old temple. Still, there is new evidence that the temple may have stood to the north where the Dome of the Rock shrine is today and that if the temple were to be rebuilt in its old place, the Dome of the Rock shrine would be in its outer courts. If this is certain, then it would explain why the angel told John, "Leave out the court which is outside the temple, and do not measure it, for it has been given to the Gentiles." Orthodox Jews believe that the Messiah will rebuild the temple, but the man they will initially embrace as their Messiah will be the antichrist: "I have come in My Father's name, and you do not receive Me; if another comes in his own name, him you will receive" (John 5:43). In the Bible we have heard of the tribulation temple in Daniel 9:26–27, Matthew 24:15–26, and 2 Thessalonians 2:3–4.

Historically and biblically, there have been two temples built in Jerusalem. One is Solomon's temple, which was destroyed by the Romans in 586 BC, and Zerubbabel's temple, later renamed Herod's temple, which Cyrus of Persia allowed to be rebuilt by the Jews in 538 BC. A third temple will be built in the tribulation, and it will be instrumental in exposing the true colors of the antichrist. At the midpoint of the seven-year tribulation, the antichrist will break the covenant with Israel, establish his "image" within the temple, and declare himself as God. This declaration is known as the "abomination of desolation" prophesied in Daniel chapters 11–31. So, Revelation 11:1–2 occurs amid the tribulation, after the temple is rebuilt, with the Gentiles overrunning the city and the temple's outer courts. These Gentiles will be followers of

Islam who have pledged their allegiance to the antichrist at this point of the tribulation, thinking he is their messiah, their savior Al-Mahdi. They have taken over Jerusalem once the persecution of Jews and Christians began at the hands of the antichrist. In contempt of the one true God and His followers, they will "tread the holy city underfoot for forty-two months."

> "And I will give power to my two witnesses, and they will prophesy one thousand two hundred and sixty days, clothed in sackcloth."

> These are the two olive trees and the two lampstands standing before the God of the earth. And if anyone wants to harm them, fire proceeds from their mouth and devours their enemies. And if anyone wants to harm them, he must be killed in this manner. These have power to shut heaven, so that no rain falls in the days of their prophecy; and they have power over waters to turn them to blood, and to strike the earth with all plagues, as often as they desire.

> Revelation 11:3–6

Now, during the first half of the tribulation, God will send "two witnesses" to witness to the Jewish people of Israel. These men have been given supernatural power from God with a ministry of judgment. They will witness for the first half of the tribulation until they are killed by the "beast from the bottomless pit" (Satan), at the midpoint when the antichrist declares himself as God and releases his fury on the people of Israel. Satan is escalating his efforts because he knows his time is near and will soon be bound for a thousand years. God's purpose during the tribulation is for Israel to recognize their Messiah (the One whom they pierced) and cry out to Him for salvation, bringing redemption to the Jews. The two witnesses' ministry is to proclaim Jesus as Lord to the Jews, and their ministry is of judgment and repentance. The two witnesses have been given power from God to call fire on their enemies. Fire proceeds from their mouths and destroys anyone who attempts to harm them. These witnesses have the power to minister their testimony for forty-two months despite the antagonism from the world. This is a time of dark and evil events with elements of hell on earth, as Satan is present in full force in his domain. The two witnesses have the power to shut the heavens; they have the power to turn the waters into blood and to strike the earth with plagues as often as they wish. They can bring drought and plague, like Moses and Elijah. These witnesses have a unique, continual empowerment from the Holy Spirit. They are mentioned in Zechariah's "olive trees and oil lamps" prophecy (Zechariah 4:2–3 and 4:14). The identity of these witnesses in Scripture has not been revealed. Still, there has been much speculation over the years. Some say they are Elijah and Elisha; some say Elijah and Moses. The book of Malachi suggests that Elijah is one of the two witnesses. Still, according to Haggai, Zerubbabel might be the other. We don't know for sure. We don't need to know if God hasn't told us.

"When they finish their testimony, the beast that ascends out of the bottomless pit will make war against them, overcome them, and kill them" (Revelation 11:7).

Once the "abomination of desolation" occurs, Satan, who possesses the antichrist ("the beast that ascends out of the bottomless pit"), will be able to overpower them and kill them. None have been able to harm them before this point, but now that their mission is fulfilled, God allows them to be slain and their bodies left on display in the street for three-and-a-half days.

"And their dead bodies will lie in the street of the great city which spiritually is called Sodom and Egypt, where also our Lord was crucified" (Revelation 11:8).

This verse refers to Jerusalem, the city where Jesus was crucified, now overrun by Gentiles and immersed in sin (Revelation 11:2). The Gentiles are most likely Islamic Muslims near the Dome of the Rock, which, during the tribulation, is on the outer courts of the newly built Jewish temple. Remember, God Himself never dwells in this temple, which has developed in the covenant between the antichrist and Israel. Now God lives inside all born-again. After Christ's sacrifice for our sins, believers received the Holy Spirit at Pentecost, making their bodies the temple of God. This is a good reason for Christians to never donate in our present time to the rebuilding of this third temple. This temple will not be a temple of Yahweh during the tribulation. Supporting it denies Christ's finished work on the cross.

> Then those from the peoples, tribes, tongues, and nations will see their dead bodies three-and-a-half days, and not allow their dead bodies to be put into graves. And those who dwell on the earth will rejoice over them, make merry, and send gifts to one another, because these two prophets tormented those who dwell on the earth.
>
> Revelation 11:9–10

The antichrist will leave the two witnesses' dead bodies on display for all to see for three-and-a-half days. In the traditions of the Middle East, it would be downright disrespectful not to bury the dead soon after their death. But the antichrist does this to disgrace and humiliate them in the eyes of the people, who will rejoice over their death in the streets. They will delight in giving gifts to each other in celebration of them being killed because these witnesses have plagued them for three-

and-a-half years, and no one has been able to stop them. The antichrist will become a magnificent hero in the eyes of the people of the earth. The witnesses will have power until they have completed their testimony and service to God. These two witnesses preaching their call to repentance tormented many because the people couldn't stand to hear the truth while they loved the lie. Deception will be widespread, making humanity vulnerable to the antichrist's lies. Only those in Christ without the cloud of delusion upon them will see the truth clearly by the power of God's seal and protection.

> Now after the three-and-a-half days the breath of life from God entered them, and they stood on their feet, and great fear fell on those who saw them. And they heard a loud voice from heaven saying to them, "Come up here." And they ascended to heaven in a cloud, and their enemies saw them. In the same hour there was a great earthquake, and a tenth of the city fell. In the earthquake seven thousand people were killed, and the rest were afraid and gave glory to the God of heaven.
>
> The second woe is past. Behold, the third woe is coming quickly.

Revelation 11:11–14

It must have been frightening to see these two witnesses, having been dead on the street for three-and-a-half days, suddenly stand up before the watching eyes of the whole world. The enemies of these witnesses must have been horrified and astounded. Still, we can easily see in this present age how an occurrence like this could be broadcast and televised for the whole world to witness. Modern-day satellite television makes it possible for this prophecy to be fulfilled. In the next verse,

God calls them home, saying, "Come up here," much like Elijah and Enoch were raptured in the Old Testament. As the world watches, they ascend to heaven in a cloud. In that same hour, a violent earthquake shook the city of Jerusalem, and a tenth of the city crumbled down, killing seven thousand people. The rest who survived were filled with fear and dropped and gave glory to God in heaven. At this point in the book of Revelation, we have not yet come to the seventh trumpet, nor have we come to the seven bowls of God's wrath to be poured out. Yet, we see tremendous catastrophes happening on the earth. Now, a great earthquake bringing judgment occurs, killing seven thousand people and causing many who survive to be afraid and give glory to God. However, we're not told if this brings them to salvation.

CHAPTER 4

THE SEVENTH AND
FINAL TRUMPET

So, now the seventh trumpet is heard. (Note: this is not the "last trumpet" referred to by Paul in 1 Corinthians 15:51–52.) Not all "trumpets" are the same; this one is called the seventh, not the last. We know from other scriptures that the rapture will occur before the "lawless one" is revealed. Second Thessalonians 2:7–8 tells us the Restrainer must be taken out of the way, "and then the lawless one will be revealed." In this epistle, Paul wrote to the Corinthian church about the rapture, the catching up of the bride of Christ. Also, when John is called to heaven by a voice sounding like a trumpet in Revelation 4:1–4, it signifies the voice of God thundering like a trumpet blast. In Revelation 11:15, however, the rapture is three-and-a-half years past, and now we are reading about the last series of judgments. It may be the last of the seven trumpets here, but not the last trumpet described in Corinthians chapter 15 that will sound at the rapture of the church. At the rapture, it will likely be the voice of the Lord Himself.

> Then the seventh angel sounded: And there were loud voices in heaven, saying, "The kingdoms of this world have become the kingdoms of our Lord and of His Christ, and He shall reign forever and ever!" And the twenty-four elders who sat before God on their thrones fell on their faces and worshiped God,

saying:

> "We give You thanks, O Lord God Almighty, The One who is and who was and who is to come, Because You have taken Your great power and reigned. The nations were angry, and Your wrath has come, And the time of the dead, that they should be judged, And that You should reward Your servants the prophets and the saints, And those who fear Your name, small and great, And should destroy those who destroy the earth."

> Then the temple of God was opened in heaven, and the ark of His covenant was seen in His temple. And there were lightnings, noises, thunderings, an earthquake, and great hail.

> Revelation 11:15–19

Now, as we return to the progression of the "trumpet judgments," the angel sounds the seventh trumpet. All the seals, trumpets, and bowls prepare the earth for the return of Jesus Christ. The seventh trumpet sounds the proclamation of the Lord's kingdom and reign on earth. The four and twenty elders, which are the saints who sat before God on their seats, fall upon their faces worshipping God, proclaiming, "We give You thanks, O Lord God Almighty, The One who is and who was and who is to come, Because You have taken Your great power and reigned" (Revelation 11:16–17). These twenty-four elders, I believe, represent the saints, all believers in Christ from the "church age," as well as the righteous believers from the Old Testament who are in heaven at this point, giving glory to God. If you've placed your trust and faith in Jesus Christ, this refers to you and I, as Christians today, before the tribulation. This thanksgiving prayer and praise of Revelation 11:16–18 isn't to thank God that He has already done this but more an announcement that the hour has come for these things to take place and that they have been permanently set in motion. They're thanking God in advance by faith that His promises are faithful and true. The wait is over; we stand at the throne, giving glory to God, and His reign is imminent! While rejoicing, the nations on earth are angry; God's wrath has come. "And the time of the dead, that they should be judged" is at hand, and the time of reward for God's servants, the prophets, the saints, and all who fear God's name small and great. God will destroy the wicked, and the saints will receive their crowns of reward. The temple of God was opened in heaven, and the heavenly ark of the covenant can be seen in the heavenly temple: "And there were lightnings, noises, thunderings, an earthquake, and great hail."

As we move into chapter 12, we are deviating from the chronological progression of the story. We will return to this progression when we come to the seven bowls (or vials) of judgment. This deviation allows for another interlude from the judgments. So, now we are taking a more descriptive view of other scenes depicting some key players of the tribulation.

"Now a great sign appeared in heaven: a woman clothed with the sun, with the moon under her feet, and on her head a garland of twelve stars. Then being with child, she cried out in labor and in pain to give birth" (Revelation 12:1–2).

We learn the woman's identity in Joseph's dream through Genesis 37:9, where the sun, moon, and eleven stars bow down to him. This is the exact figure here, but now we see twelve stars. In that dream, the sun represented Jacob, the moon represented Joseph's mother, Rachel, and the eleven stars were Israel's sons, who bowed down to Joseph. In Revelation chapter 12, the woman has twelve stars because Joseph is now among the other tribes of Israel (Ephraim and Manasseh). These passages are to be taken figuratively, not literally. John wrote it was a great sign. So, this woman will not appear verbatim on the earth. God uses this "sign" to communicate something to John and us.

In Revelation chapters 12, 13, and 14, the key figures of the great tribulation are described, and this great sign introduces the first of the seven, the "woman" representing Israel. The other prominent figures we will see as we progress through these chapters are the "dragon" representing Satan, the "man-child" representing Jesus, The "angel Michael," who is head of the angelic host, the "offspring of the woman" who represents the Gentiles who come to faith during the tribulation, the "beast out of the sea" representing the antichrist, and the "beast out of the earth" depicting the false prophet who promotes the antichrist. Beginning with this chapter, the "woman" represents the nation of Israel, those twelve tribes that came out of Jacob (Israel), and she is seen here as ready to give birth. The purpose of God for the nation of Israel was to bring the Messiah into the world. He was to be of the seed of Abraham and of the seed of David. God was working with this nation, preparing them as the instrument by which His Son would come into the world. God chose the nation of Israel for this purpose. He could have chosen any body of people for His purposes, but it pleased Him to choose Israel. God's will be done. This is why they are called the "chosen people;" they were selected to be the people God would use to bring forth His Son into the world. Tragically, when God used them for this purpose, they rejected His Son whom He sent, as they rejected the prophets before Him (Matthew 23:29–34).

> And another sign appeared in heaven: behold, a great, fiery red dragon having seven heads and ten horns, and seven diadems on his heads. His tail drew a third of the stars of heaven and threw them

to the earth. And the dragon stood before the woman who was ready to give birth, to devour her Child as soon as it was born.

Revelation 12:3–4

In the first four verses, we see two signs: the woman, Israel, ready to bring forth the Messiah (the Christ), and the dragon, ready to devour her Child (Christ Jesus) as soon as He is born. "His tail drew a third of the stars of heaven": I believe this describes a third of the angelic host who sided with Satan (his angels of Revelation 12:9). This army of celestial beings in league with him comprises the world of demonic spirits who answer to Satan, to help him deceive the world's nations. "And the dragon stood before the woman who was ready to give birth, to devour her Child as soon as it was born." When Jesus was born in Bethlehem, and the wise men visited Herod and told him the King had been born, Herod became paranoid and threatened that someone else would take his throne. He sent the wise men to Bethlehem to find the Child, but he got nervous when they didn't return. Herod had an evil heart and had killed his own wife and sons before, so he ordered all the baby boys in the area who were two years of age to be slaughtered in hopes of killing the Christ-Child. God sent an angel to Mary's husband, Joseph, in a dream, as we see in Matthew 2:12–14:

> Then, being divinely warned in a dream that they [the wise men] should not return to Herod, they departed for their own country another way.
>
> Now when they had departed, behold, an angel of the Lord appeared to Joseph in a dream, saying, "Arise, take the young Child and His mother, flee to Egypt, and stay there until I bring you word; for Herod will seek the young Child to destroy Him."

When he [Joseph] arose, he took the young Child and His mother by night and departed for Egypt, and was there until the death of Herod, that it might be fulfilled which was spoken by the Lord through the prophet, saying, "Out of Egypt I called My Son."

They remained in Egypt until the death of Herod.

"She bore a male Child who was to rule all nations with a rod of iron. And her Child was caught up to God and His throne" (Revelation 12:5).

The "Child" is obviously Jesus. This means that the woman of Revelation 12:1 cannot be the church because Jesus gives birth to the church, not the other way around. Therefore, the woman must be Mary or the nation of Israel, the only two "women" who could have given birth to Jesus. As we move on through Revelation, we see it is Israel, not Mary. We know this because the rest of Revelation chapter 12 will demonstrate that this woman is Israel. At the end of the tribulation, when Jesus comes to establish His reign and kingdom, He will rule the world with a "rod of iron" (Psalm 2:9 and Revelation 19:15). Jesus has been caught up to God and His throne, and that is where He is now in our present time. He ascended into heaven as recorded in Luke and other gospels. He is there now, sitting on His throne, advocating for us in our defense against the accusations of Satan, waiting for the Father God to put all things in subjection unto Him. So, the woman brought forth the Child. Then the Child, Jesus the Christ, after His death, burial, and resurrection, ascended to the throne of God at His Father's right hand, where He waits for God the Father to say it is time for Him to go receive His bride, the church.

"Then the woman fled into the wilderness, where she has a place prepared by God, that they should feed her there one thousand two hundred and sixty days" (Revelation 12:6).

Now, we've moved to a future event. This verse helps to understand that the woman is not Mary. It wouldn't make sense that Mary fled into the wilderness to a place prepared for her by God, but it does make sense that Israel indeed will flee to safety. "One thousand two hundred and sixty days": This reference to a three-and-a-half-year period connects these events with the final seven years, or the seventieth week, of the Daniel 9 prophecy. Since Revelation 12:5 describes the ascension of Jesus, and Revelation 12:6 describes yet-to-occur events in the seventieth week of Daniel, there must be a separation of thousands of years between these two events. In Matthew 24:15, Jesus said, "'Therefore when you see the "abomination of desolation," spoken of by Daniel the prophet, standing in the holy place' (whoever reads, let him understand)." This is what verse 12:6 in Revelation talks about: the antichrist coming to the temple, ceasing all worship of the one true God, and standing in the temple proclaiming himself to be God. So, when this happens, Jesus said to flee from where you are and not to stop for anything or go back for anything! The antichrist will turn his anger toward the Jewish people and severely persecute and murder them. They will run at the midpoint of the tribulation when the son of perdition shows his "true colors;" they will be fed by God for three-and-a-half years. Some scholars believe this will be at the rock city of Petra, southeast of the Dead Sea. God will provide and feed them, similarly to how He fed the Israelites with "manna," fed Elijah with ravens, and how Jesus fed the five thousand with five loaves and two fish. We worship an all-capable God who has and will make this happen for His chosen people.

> And war broke out in heaven: Michael and his an-
> gels fought with the dragon; and the dragon and
> his angels fought, but they did not prevail, nor was

a place found for them in heaven any longer. So the great dragon was cast out, that serpent of old, called the Devil and Satan, who deceives the whole world; he was cast to the earth, and his angels were cast out with him.

Revelation 12:7–9

At the midpoint of the tribulation, God will turn His anger toward Satan, both on earth and in heaven. A great battle will occur between Satan, his fallen angels, and the archangel Michael and his angels. The "dragon" represents Satan in this text, denoting his fierce and murderous nature. It is not a literal dragon being cast down to the earth, but a symbol like the other symbols used to represent the players in these events. "Seven diadems on his heads": This dragon has tremendous power (seven heads and ten horns) and claims royal authority (seven diadems). The diadems or crowns represent his presumptuous claims of royal supremacy against the true King, our Lord. The antichrist wants to be considered a king. This time of war in heaven is described in the first verse of Daniel chapter 12: "At that time Michael shall stand up, The great prince who stands watch over the sons of your people; And there shall be a time of trouble, Such as never was since there was a nation, Even to that time. And at that time your people shall be delivered" (Daniel 12:1).

Some individuals and groups (such as the Seventh-day Adventists and Jehovah's Witnesses) insist on saying that Michael is Jesus because "he has his angels," but this is wholly inaccurate. If Satan, a fallen angelic being, can have "his angels" in Revelation 12:7, why shouldn't Michael, an unfallen angelic being, have his angels? Some say Michael must be Jesus because he is called the archangel (Jude chapter 9), a leader or prince among the angels. They say that only Jesus is the leader of the angels. According to Daniel 10:13, 10:20, and 10:21,

Michael is one of several angelic princes. There are other archangels. Satan was an archangel named Lucifer before he fell, and Gabriel is another biblically known archangel. Jude chapter 9 says that Michael would not rebuke or accuse Satan on his own authority, but he would only say, "The Lord rebukes you." This shows that Michael is equally ranked with Satan and recognizes his position under the Lord, who is the highest in rank. So, Michael isn't Jesus because Jesus often rebuked Satan and demons in His own authority (Matthew 17:18, Mark 1:25, 9:25, Luke 4:8, 4:35). Also, Paul refers to an archangel in 1 Thessalonians 4:16 in a way that implies there are other archangels. Theologian Henry Alford wrote, "Michael is not to be identified with Christ, any more than any other of the great angels in this book. Such identification here would confuse hopelessly the actors in this heavenly scene."

This is a battle between equals. In Revelation 12:9, the dragon represents Satan, and Satan is no equal to God, for God has no equal. He is Supreme overall. Satan is equal to Michael in rank, who appears to be the chief over the angels opposite this chief of the fallen angels, Satan. Michael and his angels will fight against Satan and prevail against him. Satan will be cast out of heaven, along with his fallen angels.

> Then I heard a loud voice saying in heaven, "Now salvation, and strength, and the kingdom of our God, and the power of His Christ have come, for the accuser of our brethren, who accused them before our God day and night, has been cast down. And they overcame him by the blood of the Lamb and by the word of their testimony, and they did not love their lives to the death. Therefore rejoice, O heavens, and you who dwell in them! Woe to the inhabitants of the earth and the sea! For the devil has come down to you, having great wrath, because

he knows that he has a short time."

Revelation 12:10–12

Whoever is behind this loud voice is someone of redeemed humanity. It is not an angel or God because the voice speaks of the accuser of *our brethren*. The "accuser of our brethren" is Satan, who has been in heaven accusing us all, while our Intercessor and Advocate, Jesus, has been defending us, sitting at the right hand of the Father on the throne. But here, Satan's work of accusing ends as he is cast out of heaven. "Woe to the inhabitants of the earth and the sea!" Heaven's gain is earth's loss, for Satan is cast down, and now his wrath will be unleashed onto the world, right along with God's wrath. Satan's power is real and terrifying, not because he has conquered but because he knows he is beaten and has a short time left. He is like a wounded and ferocious cornered animal. Satan knows that in roughly three-and-a-half years, he'll be chained and banished to the "bottomless pit" for a thousand years. He's been defeated and will now take out his anger on the people of the earth at that time. The people of Israel have been severely persecuted throughout the ages, time after time. Now, they will be persecuted one last time.

> Now when the dragon saw that he had been cast to the earth, he persecuted the woman who gave birth to the male Child. But the woman was given two wings of a great eagle, that she might fly into the wilderness to her place, where she is nourished for a time and times and half a time, from the presence of the serpent.

Revelation 12:13–14

In verse 13, we are told, "He persecuted the woman who gave birth to the male Child." Some teach that the woman symbol represents all the people of God, including Israel and the church, but they promote this theory to push the idea that the church is here during the tribulation period. So, if the woman represents all the people of God (the church and faithful Israel), who are "the rest of her offspring" described in Revelation 12:17? It makes more sense to see her as Israel, the 144,000 Messianic Jews in particular. Satan now begins his attack on the Jewish people. From the time of Abraham, Israel has held a critical role in God's plan of redemption. Firstly, at the time of Abraham, it brought forth the Messiah, the Redeemer. Then, it was in the fulfillment of His plan, as we see in Matthew 23:39. In this verse, Jesus promised that the Jewish people would exist and welcome Him when He returned in glory to this world (the second coming). Israel's redemption is the tribulation's primary purpose: to be redeemed back to Christ when He reclaims the world to Himself, establishes His reign on earth, and destroys the wicked. It is not about the church because they have already been removed and are in heaven with Jesus before the tribulation began. So, Satan believes if he succeeds in destroying the Jewish people, that God's eternal plan will be in some way thwarted. Theologian John F. Walvoord said the following:

> The persecution of Israel is part of the satanic program to thwart and hinder the work of God...Israel is hated by Satan not because of any of its own characteristics but because she is the chosen of God and essential to the overall purpose of God for time and eternity.

Now we see: "But the woman was given two wings of a great eagle, that she might fly into the wilderness to her place." "Eagle's wings" is a symbol referencing the Exodus deliverance (Exodus 19:4), which also shows these people are Israel and not the church. "Where she is nourished for a time and times and half a time": This is another reference to a three-and-a-half-year period, showing that this dramatic persecution of Israel occurs during the last half of the "seventieth week of Daniel" (Daniel 9:24–27).

"So the serpent spewed water out of his mouth like a flood after the woman, that he might cause her to be carried away by the flood" (Revelation 12:15).

"The serpent spewed water out of his mouth like a flood after the woman." This describes an army that is unleashed toward the woman, Israel. The horrific fury that is unleashed against Israel by the serpent, Satan, following the "abomination of desolation" (which marks the halfway point of the seventieth week of Daniel) was referred to by Jesus in Matthew 24:15–22, when He said,

> Then let those who are in Judea flee to the mountains. Let him who is on the housetop not go down to take anything out of his house. And let him who is in the field not go back to get his clothes. But woe to those who are pregnant and to those who are nursing babies in those days! And pray that your flight may not be in winter or on the Sabbath. For then there will be great tribulation, such as has not been since the beginning of the world until this time, no, nor ever shall be. And unless those days were shortened, no flesh would be saved; but for the elect's sake those days will be shortened.

These verses speak of the tremendous fury Jesus told them to flee from. It will be directed toward "the elect," the Jewish people.

"But the earth helped the woman, and the earth opened its mouth and swallowed up the flood which the dragon had spewed out of his mouth" (Revelation 12:16).

So here is described a "great earthquake" that God invokes to swallow up the armies sent by the "serpent." In Numbers 16:30–33, God did something similar to the wicked men who had come up against Moses and Aaron. The earth opened up by the power of God and swallowed these evil men into the chasm and then closed again, and the men perished. In Revelation chapter 12, verse 16, God will do this to the armies of the antichrist.

"And the dragon was enraged with the woman, and he went to make war with the rest of her offspring, who keep the commandments of God and have the testimony of Jesus Christ" (Revelation 12:17).

Two groups are persecuted and targeted by Satan and his antichrist in the final days. In my reference to this verse above, I stated it was the 144,000 Messianic Jews who were "the rest of her offspring" whom the dragon began to persecute. But he would also persecute the Gentiles who came to Christ during the tribulation. Many from these groups will be killed and martyred for their belief and faith in our Lord Jesus Christ. Whether this begins or continues, the extreme persecution of all those who would not submit to and worship this satanic tyrant is not sure. Still, the persecution will be severe and much like war. They will be hunted down and shown no mercy. These martyrs were first introduced in Revelation 6:9–11 and Revelation 7:9–17.

In this next chapter of Revelation, we will focus on the antichrist. We will see some historical background on this man, and some believe he may already be here amidst the sea of eight billion people who populate the world today. Whoever this person is, he will not be aware of himself as the antichrist until Satan has him entirely under his power. He may not be a grown man yet; he could even be a child or a mature man in his twenties or thirties. We really don't know. He won't be revealed until the restraining church is taken out of the way. The news events of this world clearly show that we are in the "end times" and very close to the seventieth week of Daniel and what Jesus told us about in His "Olivet Discourse" (Matthew chapter 24). Though we can't set dates, we are getting close to the time of the rapture, and shortly following, the tribulation will begin. The events of the world are lined up with the signs we've been told to watch for by Jesus.

Even as I write this, Russia has been at war with Ukraine and has aligned itself with Iran and China. Iran has backed the terrorist groups that Israel is at war with and instrumented the plan of their latest attack. Iran has funded most of the terror groups in the world for many years. On October 7, 2023, Israel was attacked unexpectedly as ground troops of the terror group Hamas invaded Israel from Gaza and began murdering and kidnapping civilians, including infants, women, children, and the elderly, on the streets and in residential homes and neighborhoods. I will spare the readers the details of how these infants and children were murdered, but suffice it to say, it was heinous. It was one of the most horrendous acts that Israel has endured since the Holocaust. Other groups are threatening to join in against Israel, such as the terrorist group Hezbollah. To add hurt to injury, government officials and civilians in many countries, including America, sided with the terrorists in protests against Israel, claiming the Israelites were the oppressors.

Good is seen as evil, and evil is seen as good. The world is ready for the antichrist, and our enemy Satan doesn't even hide anymore. The world is consumed in "lawlessness" bordering on anarchy, with crime reaching an all-time high and riots happening around the globe that are being excused and welcomed by the more liberal point of view. People are being labeled as "racists" and even canceled in society for having a conservative view. Idolatry is rampant, mainly self-worship and narcissism, and worshipping Satan is open and welcomed in many parts of the world. Satan is being "glorified" by the secular world. It is made evident in movies, cartoons, books, and music.

Greed and selfishness are the way of life now in the secular world. We are seeing things happening in the world today that, fifty years ago, we would have labeled insane. Our children are under attack from the secular world, even to the point of mutilation of their bodies under the guise of mental health and healing. Governments are trying to overrule parents in the control of their children, including medical decisions where the parents are left out. Some want to give young children the right to make decisions that they are not mature enough to make yet without providing knowledge to the parents. The nuclear family structure in this country and others has been trashed by society. The world is ripe for the rise of the antichrist. This man may be already involved in politics to some degree, unknown to us presently. Still, when the time comes, the world will know him and flock to him due to his charismatic nature and their longing for a peaceful solution to the world's problems brought on by a world at war. They'll be looking for any savior because the world will be in turmoil. According to the Bible, Satan sometimes appears as an angel of light, and the antichrist will be perceived as a man of peace until he reveals his true nature at the midpoint of the tribulation. Read the following verses that describe our modern-day world:

> Because, although they knew God, they did not glorify Him as God, nor were thankful, but became futile in their thoughts, and their foolish hearts were darkened. Professing to be wise, they became fools, and changed the glory of the incorruptible God into an image made like corruptible man—and birds and four-footed animals and creeping things.

Therefore God also gave them up to uncleanness, in the lusts of their hearts, to dishonor their bodies among themselves, who exchanged the truth of God for the lie, and worshiped and served the creature rather than the Creator, who is blessed forever. Amen.

For this reason God gave them up to vile passions. For even their women exchanged the natural use for what is against nature. Likewise also the men, leaving the natural use of the woman, burned in their lust for one another, men with men committing what is shameful, and receiving in themselves the penalty of their error which was due.

And even as they did not like to retain God in their knowledge, God gave them over to a debased mind, to do those things which are not fitting; being filled with all unrighteousness, sexual immorality, wickedness, covetousness, maliciousness; full of envy, murder, strife, deceit, evil-mindedness; they are whisperers, backbiters, haters of God, violent, proud, boasters, inventors of evil things, disobedient to parents, undiscerning, untrustworthy, unloving, unforgiving, unmerciful; who, knowing the righteous judgment of God, that those who practice such things are deserving of death, not only do the same but also approve of those who practice them.

Romans 1:21–32

These verses in Romans chapter 1 certainly describe the world we live in today. For thousands of years, these things have been gradually increasing, but never before have we seen these things running rampant throughout the world, in every town, city, and country. These words, breathed by God and written by Paul almost two thousand years ago, reflect today's modern world. A large number of people have turned away from God and chosen a new "god." Christians have become a minority compared to the entire world's population, and many followers of Christ in parts of the world are being severely persecuted. It won't be too long before Christian persecution is happening in every country as the government leaders of the world move toward a one-world government and one-world religion. The "elites" of the world are already talking and planning for one "overall" government of the world. Even some influential religious leaders are pushing for one religion of the world, claiming that all the religions of the world worship the same God. Leaders of countries, the United Nations, and the Pope, have already made steps to start these things in motion. However, our God is jealous; He commands His creation to worship Him alone, the one true living God over all, the God of Abraham, Isaac, and Jacob. "Climate change" and the new "Green Deal" have become the world's new "religion," with man worshipping the creation rather than the Creator. All these things we see are ushering in the government of the antichrist. The world will be deceived, and God will let them believe the lie. Man has rejected God and has chosen a new god, "science," in place of the Creator of the heavens and the earth. They have chosen to believe the lie of "climate change" and "evolution" instead of the truth of creation. Man doesn't want the truth in today's world. They reject hearing it, so God will allow man to be deceived. He gave humanity free will, so He will allow it if people choose to turn away from God. If a person rejects the truth, God lets them believe the lie, no matter how absurd it may be. The antichrist will deceive many people. Those who refuse to consider the truth will be deluded into believing his lies.

The word "antichrist" more accurately means "instead of Christ." He is a counterfeit Christ, but many will think he is actually Jesus Christ, and they'll be deceived. He will appear impressive at first and present himself as charming, successful, and charismatic. He will appear to be a perfect leader and politician. He will be brilliant in offering his plans to better the world. He'll fool many with false promises of peace on earth. In this sense, the antichrist will be a "satanic messiah," an unholy counterfeit of the actual Christ, Jesus. Once he drops his charade at the midpoint of the tribulation, he'll demand the people of the world to take his mark and worship him. Oppression and tyranny will ensue. So now, as we move on to Revelation chapter 13, let's take a biblical look at this man of sin, the son of perdition.

CHAPTER 5

ANTICHRIST: THE BEAST

"Then I stood on the sand of the sea. And I saw a beast rising up out of the sea, having seven heads and ten horns, and on his horns ten crowns, and on his heads a blasphemous name" (Revelation 13:1).

In Revelation chapter 12, John's visions were of heaven. Now, his visions move to the earth, and he finds himself standing on a beach of sand. "And I saw a beast rising up out of the sea": the "sea" represents a great multitude of people, as when we refer to a large crowd as "a sea of people." The "beast" is someone other than Satan since John calls him a beast and not a dragon, which distinguishes him from Satan in this scripture. In this verse, The "beast" symbolizes the antichrist. The beast has "seven heads and ten horns," so although he is not Satan, he identifies with the "dragon" (Satan) who also had "seven heads and ten horns" in chapter 12. "And on his heads a blasphemous name": The seven heads of the beast are each seen with a blasphemous name against God. This speaks of the antichrist's character. He is a blasphemer who blasphemes God and is in enmity with Him. Later, in Revelation 17:9, we'll be told that the seven heads are seven mountains on which the "woman" sits. Also in chapter 17, we'll see that the woman represents "Mystery Babylon" and not Israel as it did in chapter 12. The woman is now seen by God's view as "the mother of harlots" because God considers the worship of any other "gods" but Him, the one true God, as adultery. This isn't the actual city of Babylon, but "Mystery Babylon" because she (the woman) had brought into the church many of the pagan practices of the ancient Babylon religion (idolatry, fornication, child sacrifices) whom God had cursed. Now, in chapter 13, the beast is the antichrist. The ten horns represent kings or kingdoms, and the crowns on the horns represent his rule over the federation of ten kingdoms. A ten-nation federation or coalition, ten kingdoms uniting, will arise upon the earth and be ruled by the antichrist. Three of these kingdoms will be "plucked out by the roots" by the antichrist, as we see in Daniel 7:8. The prophecies of Daniel give us a clearer understanding of the book of Revelation regarding the reign of the antichrist.

Daniel 7:7–8 reads,

> After this I saw in the night visions, and behold, a fourth beast, dreadful and terrible, exceedingly strong. It had huge iron teeth; it was devouring, breaking in pieces, and trampling the residue with its feet. It was different from all the beasts that were before it, and it had ten horns. I was considering the horns, and there was another horn, a little one, coming up among them, before whom three of the first horns were plucked out by the roots. And there, in this horn, were eyes like the eyes of a man, and a mouth speaking pompous words.

The fourth beast here in Daniel is the revised Roman Empire. During the tribulation, the Roman Empire that fell and was prominent in the days of Jesus' ministry will rise again as a powerful coalition of nations. It will crush, conquer, and destroy many smaller nations. Ten nations will be formed from this second Roman Empire, working in unison. From these, "the little horn" or antichrist will rise to power, speaking blasphemous words against God and destroying three of the ten horns, or kingdoms/nations. In Daniel 7:23–24, we see this also:

Thus he said: "The fourth beast shall be A fourth kingdom on earth, Which shall be different from all other kingdoms, And shall devour the whole earth, Trample it and break it in pieces. The ten horns are ten kings Who shall arise from this kingdom. And another shall rise after them; He shall be different from the first ones, And shall subdue three kings."

The "seven mountains" spoken of in Revelation 17:9 possibly refers to the city of Rome, also called the city of "seven hills" back in the days of the apostle John. However, there is much speculation about this amongst scholars. The federation of ten horns or kingdoms will be the "revised Roman Empire." The first three animals are a lion (in Daniel, signifying the Babylonian Empire), a bear (representing the Medo-Persian Empire), and a leopard (characterizing the Greek Empire). The fourth animal in Daniel's prophecy was an indescribable beast that shared all the horrifying characteristics of the previous beasts. This fourth beast represents the revised Roman Empire. This final world empire will be under the leadership of the antichrist, a satanically possessed, tyrannical dictator.

"Now the beast which I saw was like a leopard, his feet were like the feet of a bear, and his mouth like the mouth of a lion. The dragon gave him his power, his throne, and great authority" (Revelation 13:2).

"Now the beast which I saw": By the description given in this second verse, we can see that the "beast" is an actual man, as opposed to an empire or system of government, although he is closely identified with his world-dominating government during the tribulation. The antichrist will be worshipped as a "god," but people never worship an empire or government, so this beast must be a man. "Judas Iscariot" is called the "son of perdition" in John 17:12, as also the antichrist in 2 Thessalonians 2:3. As Judas was a man and not a government system or empire, it shows that the antichrist will also be a man with power, a throne, and great authority, given to him by Satan, the dragon. Satan's throne is here on earth, certainly not in heaven. We are told in Scripture, "The earth is the LORD's, and all its fullness, The world and those who dwell therein" (Psalm 24:1, Exodus 9:29, 1 Corinthians 10:26, 28). Everything that exists belongs to God the Creator. Although, as we see in this verse, Satan gives the antichrist "his power, his throne, and great authority," it is short-lived. All his abilities, throne, and authority will dissolve when Christ returns to the earth. Jesus will return to redeem the earth to Himself, but it has yet to happen. It will happen at the second coming at the end of the tribulation. Today, however, the earth is under the influence of Satan, who presently holds dominion over the earth and has since the fall of Adam and Eve. Jesus came in His first earthly visitation to save us from our sin, conquering "Death and Hades," and to set in motion God's plan to redeem the earth back to Himself. He owns the "title deed," the scroll with seven seals, because of His work on the cross, but He hasn't yet claimed the earth. However, He will when He returns again to the earth as the conquering Lord and King. Satan took Jesus, during His first advent on earth, onto a high mountain and showed Him all the world's kingdoms in a moment. "And the devil said to Him, 'All this authority I will give You, and their glory; for this has been delivered to me, and I give it to whomever I wish. Therefore, if You will worship before me, all will be Yours'" (Luke 4:5–7). Jesus never told him he was wrong in doing this. He just rebuked him for tempting Him, quoting the Word of God: "You shall worship the LORD your God, and Him only you shall serve" (Luke 4:8). These verses give proof that Satan holds dominion over the earth now. Further proof that the world belongs to Satan is demonstrated by the fact that the antichrist, who is yet to come in the future, will receive from the "dragon" at the time of his appearance his authority, his power, and his throne. Satan can only give what he already has allowed by God. The antichrist, while he reigns on earth during the great tribulation, will be Satan incarnate.

At the beginning of Revelation 13:2, we see the beast "was like a leopard, his feet were like the feet of a bear, and his mouth like the mouth of a lion." In Revelation chapter 13, the Lord uses imagery, as seen in Daniel chapter 7, to describe these three animals. Still, unlike Revelation chapter 13, Daniel chapter 7 used four animals or "beasts," including the beast of the final world empire, to describe the course of human government, spanning from Daniel's time until the return and reign of Jesus on the earth. In Revelation chapter 13, John presents this beast, the fourth beast of Daniel chapter 7, as the last world empire of the antichrist with the characteristics of the great empires of the past. This final world empire will have all the fierce qualities of the preceding empires, Babylonian, Medo-Persian, and Greek, with the addition of the ferocity of the Roman Empire. This is the final world government of the coming antichrist, which will ultimately be destroyed by the Lord Jesus Christ when He comes to redeem the earth back to Himself.

"And I saw one of his heads as if it had been mortally wounded, and his deadly wound was healed. And all the world marveled and followed the beast" (Revelation 13:3).

While the antichrist is in full force during his reign, apparently, there will be an assassination attempt on his life, and he will be mortally wounded. This isn't a superficial wound; it will actually kill him. However, miraculously, his wound will be healed, and he will live again. When the antichrist arrives, he will come in on a peace campaign, promoting a peace movement as a counterfeit savior. He will speak flattering words of peace, claiming he has all the answers and solutions for the chaos happening throughout the world. As he arrives, the extent of war on the planet will be beyond anything the world has ever seen previously, and the people on earth will believe they are at the point of extinction. He'll speak beautiful answers to their economic hardships, with solutions for world hunger, pestilence, and disease. This is truly a "counterfeit Christ" who even imitates Jesus in His death and resurrection. The world will believe this, adding tremendously to his fame and power. It was economic hardships that gave rise to Hitler in Germany. When government leadership has completely failed and the world's economies have fallen apart, desperate people are open to anybody who can solve their problems. In fact, they are hungry for anyone who seemingly may have the solution. The economic woes that plagued Germany in the 1940s laid the groundwork for Hitler to move in and rise to power on a campaign of false promises. These financial problems are beginning to grow throughout the world today. They are laying the foundation for the antichrist to arrive and build on. As the world's problems progress toward the start of the tribulation, people in their hopelessness and desire for peace will be the springboard upon which the antichrist will jump and come to power. However, after the antichrist turns on the world as a tyrant and abolishes his covenant with Israel while claiming he is God in their temple, there will be an assassination attempt, a mortal wound to his head, that will appear to be successful. Still, he will miraculously survive according to Revelation 13:3. There are some interesting other details about this event, described in the Old Testament prophecy of Zechariah chapter 11 as follows:

> For indeed I will raise up a shepherd in the land who will not care for those who are cut off, nor seek the young, nor heal those that are broken, nor feed those that still stand. But he will eat the flesh of the fat and tear their hooves in pieces.
>
> Woe to the worthless shepherd, Who leaves the

flock! A sword shall be against his arm And against his right eye; His arm shall completely wither, And his right eye shall be totally blinded.

Zechariah 11:16–17

In this prediction concerning the antichrist and the "mortal wound," we are told that the "sword shall be against his arm And against his right eye; His arm shall completely wither, And his right eye shall be totally blinded." God gives more details here in the prophetic vision of the prophet Zechariah. When the antichrist comes on the scene, he will be capable of performing great miracles, and some will even think he is Jesus Christ and be fooled. Those who did not believe the truth but took pleasure in unrighteousness will be condemned, as God will send them a strong delusion to believe the lie (2 Thessalonians 2:9–12). The antichrist will be a financial genius and a master diplomat. He will present very feasible answers for many of the world's problems. Realize here if you are presently a follower of Christ, believing and trusting in Him alone for your salvation, you will not be on earth when the antichrist rises to power, and you will not witness these things. You will be in heaven with Jesus, preparing to return with Him when He returns to the earth at the end of the tribulation.

Also, in 2 Thessalonians 2:7–8, we are told,

> For the mystery of lawlessness is already at work; only He who now restrains will do so until He is taken out of the way. And then the lawless one will be revealed, whom the Lord will consume with the breath of His mouth and destroy with the brightness of His coming.

As believers in Christ, there is no reason to watch for the antichrist. We'll not see him. We are supposed to be ready and watching for the return of Jesus Christ. All Christian believers, where the Restrainer now dwells, will remain on earth "until the Restrainer is taken out of the way" and "then the lawless one is revealed." The Restrainer is the spirit of God, who dwells in all true believers. It is the work of Satan to have people looking for the antichrist and trying to guess who he might be rather than watching for the return of our Lord and Savior. Jesus never told us to keep an eye out for the antichrist. We were told: "Now when these things begin to happen, look up and lift up your heads, because your redemption draws near" (Luke 21:28). He was basically telling us, "Keep watch for Me. I'm coming for you!" Just like the bridegroom in a Galilean wedding comes to retrieve his bride after preparing a place for them to live in his father's house, the Lord will also rescue His bride, the church, which is the body of Christ, before the wrath comes.

"So they worshiped the dragon who gave authority to the beast; and they worshiped the beast, saying, 'Who is like the beast? Who is able to make war with him?'" (Revelation 13:4).

"They worshipped the dragon": We would have never thought that there would be followers throughout the world who worshipped Satan, but we see it happening in today's modern world. There are actual satanic "churches," which are popping up around the globe. However, you don't have to belong to a satanic church to worship Satan. From major public events and parades to musical concerts and "half-time" shows, we see public displays of glamorized satanic images. We see Satan being glamorized in society's daily lives, without realizing it, through ordinary everyday events that used to be geared toward families previously but now have a darker tone to them. Media and entertainment venues, from movies to cartoons, are attempting to normalize and sometimes glorify our adversary Satan and his demons. From half-time shows depicting demonic themes and idolizing Satan to baseball events promoting transgender nuns mocking God in their performances, the world is being softened in their perception of evil. Books with graphic images and adult content that should be labeled porn have been published with the aim of teaching and grooming our children to have sexual intimacy at an early age. They have been snuck into school libraries, with some being discovered by parents, but who knows what else may be out there? These things are designed to desensitize the public to normalize evil in the minds of society, making wickedness seem good and godliness appear evil. There are too many to list here, but you can see what is happening around us. All these things are designed to lead people away from God and embrace everything that is not of God. It is a demonic agenda that is laying the foundation for the rise of the antichrist.

"Who is able to make war with him": The antichrist will be capable of performing many great miracles as he is empowered by Satan, and the world will marvel at his deeds. As you recall from chapter 11 of Revelation, when the "two witnesses" were present, they could destroy any who came against them and tried to harm them with fire from their mouths. They could open the heavens, bring fire, and stop rain. No one was able to prevent them from completing their mission, and they antagonized the secular world. However, when the antichrist, possessed by Satan himself, can kill them, his followers are exuberant, exalting, and marveling at his great power, declaring, "Who is like him?" and "Who is able to make war with him?" They will believe him to be all-powerful and that he cannot be conquered. They are again deceived by the lie and will think of him as a great hero.

"And he was given a mouth speaking great things and blasphemies, and he was given authority to continue for forty-two months. Then he opened his mouth in blasphemy against God, to blaspheme His name, His tabernacle, and those who dwell in heaven" (Revelation 13:5–6).

For a time, the beast will look like a winner in the eyes of the nations. When he blasphemes the Lord and speaks out against God's people, the godly will appear to be utter fools for adhering to their Christian faith. They will be perceived as losers in the eyes of the unbelieving world. Those who are attracted to the antichrist will look down on all followers of Christ, showing hatred toward them while worshipping the beast. To honor the beast is to worship the dragon because all the antichrist's power and abilities come from Satan himself. Their entire worship will be based on how mighty and unconquerable he appears. He continuously blasphemes the Lord, speaking against God and everything He stands for. His deluded followers will believe that they are wise to follow him, believing only a fool would cling to God, thus quenching any desire for God in themselves. The antichrist is a man of open blasphemy against the Lord. He exalts himself against all that is worshipped and anything that is in the name of God. He sits in the temple, declaring himself to be God while speaking blasphemies against the one true God of creation, His tabernacle, and those who dwell in heaven.

> It was granted to him to make war with the saints and to overcome them. And authority was given him over every tribe, tongue, and nation. All who dwell on the earth will worship him, whose names have not been written in the Book of Life of the Lamb slain from the foundation of the world.

> Revelation 13:7–8

The antichrist will wage all-out war on the Jews and the saints in the second half of the tribulation. He will persecute and destroy all those who are saved in Christ if they won't turn and worship him. We are told he will rule and reign over all of the families of the earth, the tongues, and the nations. In other words, the entire population of the world. This war with the saints is also predicted in the book of Daniel (Daniel 7:21, 25, and 8:24). Revelation 13:7 reveals the focus of his persecution. In his effort to defeat the cause of God's people on this earth, the antichrist's "government of the beast" will persecute, hunt down, and destroy all those who do not take his mark and bow down in worship to the beast. Again, these saints are not the "church" but God's people who have come to Christ during the seven-year tribulation. In Matthew 16:18, Jesus told Peter, "And I also say to you that you are Peter, and on this rock I will build My church, and the gates of Hades shall not prevail against it." Suppose this group of saints will be overcome by Satan. In that case, this cannot be the New Testament church that Jesus spoke of to Peter when He said, "On this rock I will build My church, and the gates of Hades shall not prevail against it." The antichrist prevails against these "saints" mentioned in Revelation 13:7, and we also know that the church saints are already in heaven with Jesus. So, these must be the "tribulation" saints who have received Jesus Christ as Lord and Savior while on earth during the reign of the antichrist. He has the power to kill whom he chooses during his reign, and he will put to death those who have placed their trust in Jesus Christ. However, to be martyred is preferable to submitting to the beast's authority or worshipping him; as we discover in the next chapter, if anyone worships him, they will lose any chance of salvation forever. "All who dwell on the earth will worship him, whose names have not been written in the Book of Life of the Lamb slain from the foundation of the world" (Revelation 13:8).

The "Book of Life" records everyone who has not rejected Christ in the world but received Him for salvation. Some say all of mankind's names are written in the Book of Life at conception, and if we choose God through Christ and not reject our Lord and Savior, our names will remain. Psalm 69:28 reads, "Let them be blotted out of the book of the living, And not be written with the righteous." This certainly implies the names are already in the book but will be "blotted out" upon man's rejection of Christ. In that case, your name will "not be written" along with the righteous at the time of judgment. But we really don't know for sure because in 13:8, it reads, "Have not been written," which implies it is only written upon receiving Christ as Savior. So, we won't know this small detail of scripture translation unless God reveals it to us at another time. However, we know you won't have your name in the Book of Life if you willingly worship the beast. In the verse, "the Lamb slain from the foundation of the world," this meaningful reference to Jesus (the Lamb slain) reminds us that God's plan of redemption was set in place before He created any who would be redeemed. God was not caught off guard by Adam's fall nor surprised by any human frailty to sin today. It is all going according to God's great plan. (Also see Matthew 25:34, John 17:24, Ephesians 1:4, and 1 Peter 1:20.)

"If anyone has an ear, let him hear. He who leads into captivity shall go into captivity; he who kills with the sword must be killed with the sword. Here is the patience and the faith of the saints" (Revelation 13:9–10).

The dispensation of grace has ended, and the Lord, through John, admonishes a stern warning here. All those who wield the "sword" of the beast against God's people will be severely dealt with in kind. Those who live by the sword will die by the sword. Those who hunt down and persecute Christians and make them captives will soon be placed into captivity themselves. However, "captivity" for the wicked entails separation from God and eternal torment in the lake of fire. This will occur following the great white throne judgment, in which your captivity will never end in the lake of fire, known as the "second death." There is no escape from the torment of the lake of fire, so they will genuinely be captives there. We then see, "Here is the patience and the faith of the saints." These verses are a word of encouragement to those who will experience these terrible persecutions from the antichrist. The suffering and death they will have to endure for their faith as martyrs will be avenged by God Himself. Their patience will be rewarded by their assured inheritance in Christ Jesus, by their faith. This is the blessed hope of eternity in the presence of God, as His children, in the bliss and wonder of heaven and earth.

> Then I saw another beast coming up out of the earth, and he had two horns like a lamb and spoke like a dragon. And he exercises all the authority of the first beast in his presence, and causes the earth and those who dwell in it to worship the first beast, whose deadly wound was healed.

> Revelation 13:11–12

This introduces the third member of hell's unholy trinity. A demonic and twisted counterfeit of the Holy Spirit who glorifies Christ. However, this false holy man's mission is to "falsely glorify" the antichrist through lies and wonders to bring people to worship the beast. As a counterfeit trinity, the dragon is the anti-Father, the beast rising from the sea is the anti-Christ, and the beast rising from the earth is the anti-Holy Spirit. This beast coming out of the earth is the "false prophet." He will be the leader of the one-world religious system. He could be a well-known evangelist, an ayatollah, a guru, or even a pope. Still, many will hear his lies and flock toward the antichrist. The scripture here says he came up "out of the earth," which differentiates him from the antichrist, who came up "out of the sea." He will appear differently than the antichrist, appearing more like a "lamb" than a beast, deceiving many. Because he is a "religious" man, people will be fooled and cling to everything he says, as he deceivingly portrays the antichrist as a "savior" performing great miracles. The beast from the earth is a satanic prophet who entices the world through miracles and deception to worship the beast and the dragon.

> He performs great signs, so that he even makes fire
> come down from heaven on the earth in the sight
> of men. And he deceives those who dwell on the
> earth by those signs which he was granted to do in
> the sight of the beast, telling those who dwell on
> the earth to make an image to the beast who was
> wounded by the sword and lived.
>
> Revelation 13–14

The natural man has an unquestionable religious impulse,
but they also have an unquestionable rebellion against God.
Men don't necessarily want to eliminate religion; they want
their own religion. Most, but not all, say they want heaven, but
they don't want God in it.

Theologian Matthew Henry writes,

> Lying wonders, pretended miracles, by which they
> should be deceived, and prevailed with to worship
> the former beast in this new image or shape that
> was now made for him; they would pretend to bring
> down fire from heaven, as Elias did, and God some-
> times permits his enemies, as he did the magicians
> of Egypt, to do things that seem very wonderful,
> and by which unwary persons may be deluded. It is
> well known that the papal kingdom has been long
> supported by pretended miracles.

The false prophet will be given power by Satan to perform
"miracles," such as bringing fire down from heaven as Elijah
had done. Not all miracles performed are proof that one is of
God. Theologian Joseph Seiss wrote,

There is a supernatural power which is against God and truth, as well as one for God and truth. A miracle, simply as a work of wonder, is not necessarily of God. There has always been a devilish supernaturalism in the world, running alongside of the supernaturalism of divine grace and salvation.

So, these miracles performed by the "false prophet" and his appearance as a "religious" man will help lend authenticity to his deception. The deluded people will believe he is a prophet of God. Jesus said that in the end times, false prophets would emerge and show great signs and wonders to deceive many (Matthew 24:24). Jesus also said that some who worked miracles, even in His name, were false followers and would perish in hell (Matthew 7:22–23).

Speaking of the false prophet, Matthew Henry (1662–1714) wrote,

All agree that this must be some great impostor, who, under a pretense of religion, shall deceive the souls of men. The papists would have it to be Apollonius Tyranaeus, but Dr. More has rejected that opinion and fixes it upon the ecclesiastical powers of the papacy. The pope shows the horns of a lamb, pretends to be the vicar of Christ upon earth, and so to be vested with his power and authority; but his speech betrays him, for he gives forth those false doctrines and cruel decrees which show him to belong to the dragon, and not to the Lamb.

This doesn't give value to asserting that the false prophet must be the pope. However, it could be someone very much like him. The pope of our present age has already stated that all religions worship the same God in his attempts to promote a one-world religion. As of the following verse, "Telling those who dwell on the earth to make an image to the beast who was wounded by the sword and lived," the false prophet uses this as leverage and points people toward the fact that the antichrist basically "died and rose again," leading them to falsely believe he is "the Christ returned" and persuades them to make an "image" of the beast to be worshipped. This image will be the epitome of all idolatry in the world.

> He was granted power to give breath to the image of the beast, that the image of the beast should both speak and cause as many as would not worship the image of the beast to be killed. He causes all, both small and great, rich and poor, free and slave, to receive a mark on their right hand or on their foreheads, and that no one may buy or sell except one who has the mark or the name of the beast, or the number of his name. Here is wisdom. Let him who has understanding calculate the number of the beast, for it is the number of a man: His number is 666.

> Revelation 13:15–18

"He was granted power to give breath to the image of the beast, that the image of the beast should both speak and cause as many as would not worship the image of the beast to be killed." The arrival of "artificial intelligence" or "AI" in today's world has burst onto the world scene. Robotics are being studied and developed in the world today as well, and both of these scientific firsts are being designed to combine them into a single unit at a fantastic rate of progress. Such is the goal of the financial elites of this world. John had no idea in his day when he saw the visions God gave him, just what these verses could mean, but in today's world, these things make much more sense. It is pretty feasible that when the antichrist is in the world during the tribulation, the "image" spoken of here could be a scientific reality of "AI" and "robotics," combined with the supernatural power of Satan. This would allow the image to seem alive and even speak. "He causes all, both small and great, rich and poor, free and slave, to receive a mark on their right hand or on their foreheads, and that no one may buy or sell except one who has the mark or the name of the beast, or the number of his name."

There has been much speculation about the "mark of the beast" and the number 666 over the years. Horror films have used it often; you see it in tattoos, comics, graphic novels, and even record albums that have portrayed it to denote something evil, demonic, or scary. However, no one knows what it will be during the reality of the tribulation, other than it will represent and belong to the antichrist and distinguish the bearer of the mark as a worshipper of him. The number somehow relates to the antichrist himself, but many have tried to decipher its meaning to no avail. It could even be something as ordinary as a "bar code," for all we know. Still, we do know the antichrist will insist on the people of the earth taking this mark as a symbol of their worship of him, and the only way you'll be able to buy or sell will be to choose him over God. We are given a sincere and stern warning by God, however, that if you receive this mark, you've condemned yourself to eternal damnation, and you will never see the kingdom of heaven. If you are on earth during this terrible time, you'll have to make a choice between God or the antichrist. To choose God during the "great tribulation" will more than likely ensure your death at the hands of the antichrist and his tyranny. To hold to Christ, you probably will be "martyred" for your faith if you are living during the tribulation.

CHAPTER 6

THE 144,000

So now, as we continue, John is given a vision of the Lord standing on Mount Zion with the 144,000.

> Then I looked, and behold, a Lamb standing on Mount Zion, and with Him one hundred and forty-four thousand, having His Father's name written on their foreheads. And I heard a voice from heaven, like the voice of many waters, and like the voice of loud thunder. And I heard the sound of harpists playing their harps. They sang as it were a new song before the throne, before the four living creatures, and the elders; and no one could learn that song except the hundred and forty-four thousand who were redeemed from the earth. These are the ones who were not defiled with women, for they are virgins. These are the ones who follow the Lamb wherever He goes. These were redeemed from among men, being firstfruits to God and to the Lamb. And in their mouth was found no deceit, for they are without fault before the throne of God.
>
> Revelation 14:1–5

The 144,000 are the same 144,000 we saw in chapter 7 of Revelation. We were told then that God instructed the angel not to harm the earth until the 144,000 were sealed. Once they were sealed on their foreheads, no harm would come to them by the hand of God. In these passages, we now learn what the seal is; it is the name of God, Yahweh, on their foreheads. No matter how you pronounce it, it is the name of the Almighty, one true living God, the Creator Lord, God the Father, God the Son, God the Holy Spirit. Some pronounce this "Yah-Way," and some pronounce His name as "YeHoWah," or transliterated "Jehovah," with the *Y* sounding like a *J*. The *W* sounds like a *V*. Some transliterated His name as YHWH, but the Jews who do not read this as Adonai (the Lord) read it as Ha-Shem (The Name). I've heard some equate the audible YHWH with the spirit of life God breathed into Adam at creation. They relate this to our breathing, with "YH" being the sound of a breath in and "WH" being the sound of a breath out so that we are exclaiming the name of the Lord with every breath we take. YHWH is the Godhead: God the Father, God the Son, and God the Holy Spirit, three persons, one God. This was the name the 144,000 were sealed with on their foreheads to protect them. They are seen here standing triumphantly with the Lord, with these seals on their foreheads, which tells us that God had saved them and survived the tribulation. Satan was unable to touch them. This seal announces that these young Jewish, celibate men belong to our God in heaven. The antichrist demanded everyone to have his "mark" on their foreheads or hands, and his mark is just another counterfeit version of God's seal, as the antichrist tries to imitate all that God does. Satan, who controls the antichrist, in his pride and vanity, believes he is equal to God, which he is not, so he displays a counterfeit version of God's plan. God's seal on the foreheads of the 144,000 was for their protection from harm, much like Shadrach, Meshach, and Abed-Nego were protected from the fiery furnace by God in Daniel 3:19–25. In Daniel, the on-lookers outside saw three men thrown into the furnace, but four men standing in the flames. The Lord was with them in the fire and shows us, just like the 144,000 here, proof that God is quite capable of protecting and preserving His people as He wills. Then John hears a voice from heaven: "Like the voice of many waters, and like the voice of loud thunder," which by its description clearly shows us that this is the voice of God. "They sang as it were a new song before the throne...no one could learn that song except the hundred and forty-four thousand." Pastor Chuck Smith, in his commentary on these verses, writes,

> Now, they are there and they are singing an exclusive song. They have an exclusive relationship with the Lord. They were sealed and they were preserved during a portion of the great tribulation period. And so they have that special relationship with God and they can sing of that special relationship.
>
> In the same token we the church have a special relationship and we have our own song that no one can sing, except the church. Our song is the song of redemption through the blood of Jesus Christ, and we find it back in chapter five. And they sang a new song saying, "Worthy is the Lamb to take the scroll and loose the seals, for he was slain, and has redeemed us by his blood out of all the nations, tongues, tribes and people, and has made us unto our God kings and priests and we shall reign with him upon the earth" (Revelation 5:13). That is a song exclusive for the church. The one hundred and forty-four thousand cannot sing that song. They have got their own.
>
> We find the martyred saints have their own song in chapter seven. The poor angels are left out of all of these songs. They can only join the chorus.

"Worthy is the Lamb to receive glory, and honor, and power, and dominion, and authority and might and all." They can join the chorus, but they can't sing the verse. That is ours, the worthiness of the Lamb who has redeemed us by his blood. It is a song of redemption belonging to the church.

Now, these have their own songs. We can't join in, but we can listen as they declare the greatness of God and the preservation during the time of great tribulation.

So, because we see these 144,000 with Jesus on Mount Zion, some theologians disagree on the location. Some say they are in the earthly Zion, while others believe they are in the heavenly Zion. I tend to think they are in heaven at this time because they are singing their new song before the throne and before the "four living creatures," which certainly indicates they are, at this point, now in heaven. They have completed their mission on earth serving our Lord, and as the "two witnesses" were protected by God until their mission was fulfilled, so too the sealed 144,000 have left the horrors and destruction upon the earth to be rewarded by the glorious presence of God and the heavenly peace of being with Jesus forever. In the verse, "And in their mouth was found no deceit, for they are without fault before the throne of God." The 144,000 Jewish men have been deemed "righteous" by God in His sight. They have not sinned carnally nor committed spiritual adultery against God like Abraham was deemed righteous by God for his belief in His promises. The church is deemed righteous by faith and trust in Jesus' sacrifice, so too may these men, sealed with the name of God, approach their heavenly Father on the throne without fault as children of God. In Jude 1:24, it is written, "Now to Him who is able to keep you from stumbling, And to present you faultless Before the presence of His glory with exceeding joy." When the Lord presents you before the Father, He will present you faultless. In Christ, we are righteous in the eyes of our Father God because of Jesus' work on the cross. He sees us through the blood of Christ that "cleanses us from all sin" (1 John 1:7) by Jesus' sacrifice. Although our bodies are sinful, God sees us as fully justified and righteous through the blood of Jesus Christ.

> Then I saw another angel flying in the midst of heaven, having the everlasting gospel to preach to those who dwell on the earth—to every nation, tribe, tongue, and people—saying with a loud voice, "Fear God and give glory to Him, for the hour of His judgment has come; and worship Him who made heaven and earth, the sea and springs of water."

> Revelation 14:6–7

In Jesus' Olivet Discourse, given to His disciples about the end times, we read, "And this gospel of the kingdom will be preached in all the world as a witness to all the nations, and then the end will come" (Matthew 24:14). He referred to the evangelizing angel of Revelation 14:6, who would preach the gospel during the "great tribulation." The two witnesses and the 144,000 have preached the gospel, and now this angel is preaching to everyone on the earth. It is a literal angelic being. God wants everyone to repent and turn to Him before it is too late. When Jesus spoke to His disciples and said the gospel shall be preached as a witness to all nations, it referred to this angel flying in the midst of heaven declaring the everlasting gospel to all the nations and peoples of the world. The angel tells people that the hour of judgment has arrived and instructs them to fear and give glory to God and to worship the One who made the heavens and the earth and all creation. Many people these days worship "the creation" rather than "the Creator" Himself, denying He even exists. But God will make it very clear during the tribulation that this belief is false. Everyone will know that He is the Sovereign Lord and the only One worthy of their worship. One day, all will give glory to God. Philippians 2:9–11 says,

> Therefore God also has highly exalted Him and given Him the name which is above every name, that at the name of Jesus every knee should bow, of those in heaven, and of those on earth, and of those under the earth, and that every tongue should confess that Jesus Christ is Lord, to the glory of God.

It is much better to give glory to God now, worshiping Him willingly in this life, than to be induced to give Him glory later, at the great white throne judgment (Revelation 20:11–15).

"And another angel followed, saying, 'Babylon is fallen, is fallen, that great city, because she has made all nations drink of the wine of the wrath of her fornication'" (Revelation 14:8).

This angel declares that Babylon has fallen. Babylon represents mankind in organized rebellion against God. Theologian John F. Walvoord wrote, "Prophetically, 'Babylon' sometimes refers to a literal city, sometimes to a religious system, sometimes to a political system, all stemming from the evil character of historic Babylon."

We are told that Babylon has led all nations into fornication, but this is not literal. God sees it as "spiritual fornication," or adultery against God in the worship of false idols. Spiritual fornication, however, is often accompanied by literal immorality. Leading up to and into the tribulation, man, in his sinful pride and his pursuit of selfish desires at the expense of others, has been worshiping themselves rather than God, and this, too, is spiritual adultery and the worship of a false idol. To worship anyone or anything other than God Himself is idolatry or, as stated in verse 8, spiritual fornication. It is literally being unfaithful toward God. When we get to chapter 17 of Revelation, we will examine Babylon much further.

CHAPTER 7

THE MARK AND THE MARTYRS

Then a third angel followed them, saying with a loud voice, "If anyone worships the beast and his image, and receives his mark on his forehead or on his hand, he himself shall also drink of the wine of the wrath of God, which is poured out full strength into the cup of His indignation. He shall be tormented with fire and brimstone in the presence of the holy angels and in the presence of the Lamb. And the smoke of their torment ascends forever and ever; and they have no rest day or night, who worship the beast and his image, and whoever receives the mark of his name."

Revelation 14:9–11

Within these verses, we are again given a stern warning from God. To receive the mark of the beast is declaring your worship of the antichrist, and having heard the angels' proclamation, the people left on earth will have no excuse for worshipping the enemy. Mankind, during the great tribulation, will have to willingly choose the mark rather than choosing to worship the Lord their God. No one can claim ignorance by delivering this warning to the world through His angelic messenger. However, despite this, most people are still unaware of the gravity of their actions and the resulting consequences. Remember, the Word of God is perceived as foolishness to the world. In the eyes of the deceived populace, it will seem like an innocent gesture, more like a "pledge of allegiance" given to this new world leader. They won't realize that they will be actually worshiping Satan. The non-believing world of today glorifies Satan through imagery, fashion, and entertainment. They don't understand what they are doing spiritually because they don't have the Holy Spirit to guide them into all truth. We must pray for the unbelievers continually. They've rejected any belief in the Living God, so they don't think Satan exists either. They've been deceived. During the tribulation, those who reject the true Christ and take the mark willingly will be in willful rebellion against God, declaring their worship of the antichrist. Those who serve him have been deceived into thinking that in the final conflict that will soon take place, Satan and the forces of darkness will be able to overcome the forces of light. This is the foolishness of non-believing mankind and the deception of Satan. By taking the "mark," mankind will condemn themselves to the "second death." They'll be cast into the lake of fire because their names will be erased from the "Book of Life."

The truth that God holds a cup of wrath, which He makes those under judgment drink, is given numerous times in the Bible. We see in Jeremiah 51:7 that: "Babylon was a golden cup in the Lord's hand, That made all the earth drunk. The nations drank her wine; Therefore the nations are deranged." And Jeremiah 25:15 reads, "For thus says the Lord God of Israel to me: 'Take this wine cup of fury from My hand, and cause all the nations, to whom I send you, to drink it.'" In Psalm 75:8, we are told, "For in the hand of the Lord there is a cup, And the wine is red; It is fully mixed, and He pours it out; Surely its dregs shall all the wicked of the earth Drain and drink down." Still, God desires everyone to have every opportunity to be saved. This is why the gospel is being proclaimed at this final chance for salvation during the great tribulation. There is still an opening to avoid condemnation and be saved, or God would not proclaim it. Repentance is the key to salvation. Those who are "hard-hearted" will drink the wine of His passionate anger (Greek: *thymos*) and drink from the cup of God's indignation (Greek: *orge*) to be poured out. The word "indignation" is more of an extreme displeasure with someone or something. It is often used to describe God's displeasure with unrighteousness in the New Testament. But God's wrath will be a more passionate anger directed at the wicked at heart during the tribulation. The Greek word *orge* is used throughout the Bible to describe God's indignant anger, an ongoing anger toward sin and unrighteousness. The Greek word *thymos*, however, is used ten times in the book of Revelation, wherein the wrath of God is more personal and passionate, with the Lord raging His anger against those who refuse to repent. Instead of turning to God, they choose to reject His love and worship evil. As to the last verse, "And the smoke of their torment ascends forever and ever; and they have no rest day or night, who worship the beast and his image, and whoever receives the mark of his name." John F. Walvoord writes,

> In describing the worshippers of the beast, the word worship as well as the word receive in verse 11 is in the present tense emphasizing continued worship of the beast over a long period of time… the same present tense is used in describing their torment. As the worship of the beast is not interrupted by repentance, so their torment is not interrupted when repentance is too late.

The torment of the lake of fire will last for all eternity with no reprieve for all who reject God's gift of salvation.

> Here is the patience of the saints; here are those who keep the commandments of God and the faith

of Jesus.

> Then I heard a voice from heaven saying to me, "Write: 'Blessed are the dead who die in the Lord from now on.'"
>
> "Yes," says the Spirit, "that they may rest from their labors, and their works follow them."
>
> Revelation 14:12–13

Now, at this point on the timeline of the tribulation, men will have to be martyred to stay true to their faith in Christ Jesus. We see a strong contrast between the saints who will have "rest" and the wicked who will have continual torment. Patient endurance and faithfulness to God and His Word bring the reward of rest in Christ, as opposed to eternal torment without Christ. We don't know what comfort this passage will give the frightened and persecuted saints during the great tribulation. But God wants to encourage them to be faithfully steadfast in their moment of trial, even to their own physical deaths, remaining focused on the blessed reward that awaits them all eternity.

> Then I looked, and behold, a white cloud, and on the cloud sat One like the Son of Man, having on His head a golden crown, and in His hand a sharp sickle. And another angel came out of the temple, crying with a loud voice to Him who sat on the cloud, "Thrust in Your sickle and reap, for the time has come for You to reap, for the harvest of the earth is ripe." So He who sat on the cloud thrust in His sickle on the earth, and the earth was reaped.
>
> Revelation 14:14–16

Now, the moment has come for Jesus to claim what is

rightfully His: "And on the cloud sat One like the Son of Man, having on His head a golden crown." This verse clearly represents our Lord, Jesus Christ. John sees "One like the Son of Man having…a golden crown," which confirms that it is Christ. Some people struggle with Jesus being the One here who is about to harvest because of the verse, "Another angel came out of the temple, crying with a loud voice to Him who sat on the cloud." They feel that this angel wouldn't be telling the Lord, "Thrust in Your sickle and reap, for the time has come for You to reap, for the harvest of the earth is ripe," so they conclude that this "One like the Son of Man" must be another angel. But that's not so. This angel is not directing Jesus to do this. It is God who sends forth His angels to reap on His behalf. The angel is sent when the time is right, most likely by God the Father to signal the Son that the time to reap is at hand. As a battle shout from an army to their general, the angel proclaims it is time to do what they've been waiting on God to do: to reap the wheat and the tares from the earth, much like an army would cry out in support as they were about to go forth and enter into battle following their leader. A general in the military guides his soldiers to do what he commands; they are his instruments to carry out his orders. The general gives the orders, and the soldiers carry them out. This angel was not equal to the One who sat on the cloud; he was subservient to Him while giving his proclamation. The angel here proclaimed to all that the "harvest of the earth is ripe" and that the time had come for our Lord to reap the earth of its wickedness and claim it back to His ownership. The angels are God's messengers, and like a general to his soldiers, the Lord will do the reaping through His angels, who will carry it out. This angel joyously worshipped and served the Lord for what only Himself could command. As for the "golden crown," although Jesus had worn a "crown of thorns" while dying for us on the cross, He now wears a golden crown of victory, denoting His victory won in conflict as God the Son. The Greek word used here is *stephanos*, which is a victor's crown, not "diadem," which is the crown of a king. When Jesus rides back on His white horse to begin His reign on earth with the angels and saints in tow on their steeds behind Him, He will wear the crown of a king (diadem). Famous Pastor and Theologian C. H. Spurgeon wrote,

> How different it will be to see him with a crown of gold upon his head from what it was to see him wearing that terrible crown of thorns which the cruel soldiers plaited, and thrust upon his brow! The word used here does not usually refer to the diadem of power, but to the crown won in conflict; and it is very remarkable that it should be said that, when Christ comes to judge the world, he will wear the garland of victory, the crown which he has won in the great battle which he has fought. How significant of his final triumph will that crown of gold be about those brows that were once covered with bloody sweat when he was fighting the battle for our salvation!

The Greek word for "ripe," used here in these verses, denotes something that is "overripe" and ready for harvest with no delay. The earth's harvest is long overdue and literally "bursting at the seams" in woe and misery. This ancient Greek word means "to become dry or withered," so the earth will be reaped when it is "overripe" for judgment. God has waited as long as He could to allow many to come to Christ, which shows us that in His loving grace and mercy, He is not anxious to judge the world. His long-suffering patience throughout the age of mankind has given humanity plenty of time to recognize their rejection of God and repent and return to Him. Joseph Seiss wrote, "It must be remembered that evil has its harvest as well as good. There is a harvest of misery and woe—a harvest for the gathering, binding, and burning of the tares—as well as for the gathering of the wheat into the garner of heaven."

Humanity had come to the fullness of rebellion against God who created them, so now, the time has come for God to judge the world and reap the harvest.

> Then another angel came out of the temple which is in heaven, he also having a sharp sickle.
>
> And another angel came out from the altar, who had power over fire, and he cried with a loud cry to him who had the sharp sickle, saying, "Thrust in your sharp sickle and gather the clusters of the vine of the earth, for her grapes are fully ripe." So the angel thrust his sickle into the earth and gathered the vine of the earth, and threw it into the great winepress of the wrath of God. And the winepress was trampled outside the city, and blood came out of the winepress, up to the horses' bridles, for one thousand six hundred furlongs.
>
> Revelation 14:17–20

By this time, the world's nations will have gathered for a final conflict, seeking to overthrow the Lord upon His return. In Psalm 2:1, God said, "Why do the nations rage, And the people plot a vain thing? The kings of the earth set themselves, And the rulers take counsel together, Against the Lord and against His Anointed." What does God mean when He says, "The people plot a vain thing"? Well, the nations believe in their vanity that they could actually overthrow Jesus Christ and prohibit Him from coming and establishing His reign! Knowing that He is coming again to that area, they will gather together, and they will believe that they can overthrow Him. The nations of people on earth have "plotted a vain thing" because they have gathered together, in vain futility, against the Almighty Lord and against His Christ. This is the prideful vanity of Satan and the foolishness of man in their belief that they could actually overthrow God. God laughs at the thought.

When the Lord of lords and King of kings comes against this colossal gathering of armies from every nation, He will crush their attempt with one word from the "sharp sword" of His mouth (Revelation 19:21). The "battlefield," if you can even call this a battle, will be filled with their blood as deep as a horse's bridle for the length of one thousand six hundred furlongs, roughly two hundred miles. The battle will be over before the wicked even realizes it has started. This is commonly referred to as the battle of Armageddon (Revelation 16:16). It is the name used for where the nation's armies will gather for their final battle against the Lord. However, the actual battle will take place in Jerusalem. The word "Armageddon" is derived from the Hebrew language, *Har-Megiddo*: *Har* means "mount," and *Megiddo* is a city on the west side of the Jezreel Valley in Israel. "Jezreel" means "God sows," currently, it is a highly fertile area, providing some of the best produce to Israel and other parts of the world. We will get more into this battle in its description of the second coming of Jesus Christ, as detailed in chapter 19 of Revelation.

CHAPTER 8

SEVEN ANGELS WITH SEVEN BOWLS

As we move onward on the timeline of the tribulation, we come to the intro of the last seven plagues to be poured out by God. These are the "bowl" or "vial" judgments. Some translations call these "bowls," while others call them "vials;" however, these are the same judgments. They will be the fiercest of God's wrath so far to be poured out on the earth and the wicked, by which God's judgment will be completed upon the earth. The world prepared for the millennial reign of Jesus Christ.

Then I saw another sign in heaven, great and marvelous: seven angels having the seven last plagues, for in them the wrath of God is complete.

And I saw something like a sea of glass mingled with fire, and those who have the victory over the beast, over his image and over his mark and over the number of his name, standing on the sea of glass, having harps of God. They sing the song of Moses, the servant of God, and the song of the Lamb, saying: "Great and marvelous are Your works, Lord God Almighty! Just and true are Your ways, O King of the saints! Who shall not fear You, O Lord, and glorify Your name? For You alone are holy. For all nations shall come and worship before You, For

Your judgments have been manifested."

Revelation 15:1–4

John sees here a third sign that is given to him. The first sign he was given was the woman (Israel) about to give birth to the Child (Christ), which we saw in Revelation chapter 12:1–4. The second was the great red dragon waiting to devour her Child as soon as He was born in Revelation 12:3–5. In John's description of his awe-inspiring vision and the sign he saw, he uses the word "marvelous." Many people use this word today to describe something beautiful or enjoyable. Still, the term "marvelous" is derived from the verb "marvel," as in the phrase "something to marvel at." So, these seven angels, having the seven most severe plagues to be unleashed so far, were nothing for him to smile about. He meant it as something to be marveled at by the plague's size, intensity, and power. "Astonishing" might have been a better word for the translation, but the translators chose "marvelous." John sees a lot going on here in this vision. After witnessing the seven seals and the seven trumpets plagues, he now envisions the most severe of all: the seven bowl judgments about to be poured out. John tells us that when these plagues are poured out, the wrath of God will be complete, which no doubt was a relief to John after what he has already witnessed.

Still, though saddened by all he had witnessed, he clearly understood the reasoning of God's judgment upon the world. Now he sees a "sea of glass mingled with fire," much like in Revelation chapter 4 verse 6 when he saw the throne and the four living creatures there. Only now, something is added. The martyrs who stood firm in their faith to their deaths are now standing on the sea of glass, having harps, singing the song of Moses and the song of the Lamb. These are the martyrs of the tribulation, now in heaven and safe. They remained faithful to God despite the tumultuous attack of the antichrist to get them to turn. They now have the reward for their steadfast devotion to Christ. Their song is one of praise to the living God Most High! Many don't realize that the Torah, written by Moses, were books written in the format of songs. All of the Torah, the first five books of the Holy Bible, were presented as Hebrew songs of praise and the deliverance of God's people. Here, the martyred saints of the tribulation sing a similar song of praise, giving glory to God, who has brought them deliverance and salvation through the Lord, Jesus Christ, who is the Lamb. Moses' song was a result of God's deliverance of Israel from physical bondage, and the Lamb's song resulted from being delivered from spiritual bondage. While the song of Moses looks forward to the promised land across the Jordan in Israel, the song of the Lamb awaits the eternal kingdom where the Savior will reign from His throne. As we saw previously, before each series of judgments, a song of praise burst forth in heaven, giving glory to God on the throne. Now, before the bowl judgments, we find the same thing happening. A heavenly choir of saints, angels, and living creatures erupt in song, praising God and worshipping Him in heaven. A song of praise and worship always breaks out in heaven before God unleashes any judgment on the world. They sing, "Just and true are Your ways, O King of the saints!" giving glory to God. Many in today's world find objection to the portion of the Bible that shows God's wrath being poured out onto the earth. In their minds, they try to lessen the severity of it, imagining God could never be that harsh. However, God's wrath may be even more intense than we can guess from the picture Jesus gives us in the book of Revelation. In truth, as horrible as it will be on earth, it will still be far less than man deserves during the tribulation. Man chose to believe Satan rather than God in the garden, and subsequently, we became cursed and condemned to die. But then the Father sent His only begotten Son.

"And after all that has come upon us for our evil deeds and

for our great guilt, since You our God have punished us less than our iniquities deserve, and have given us such deliverance as this" (Ezra 9:13).

Because God is just and righteous, He must deal with sin in the world. Man has sinned against God, and a price must be paid. The wages of sin are paid by man himself or by substitutionary atonement provided by our Savior. It is man's choice to decide. God's justice is fair because He has provided us with a Redeemer to atone for our sins. Salvation is ours by believing.

"The LORD is merciful and gracious, Slow to anger, and abounding in mercy" (Psalm 103:8).

Now John sees seven angels coming forth from the throne of God.

> After these things I looked, and behold, the temple of the tabernacle of the testimony in heaven was opened. And out of the temple came the seven angels having the seven plagues, clothed in pure bright linen, and having their chests girded with golden bands. Then one of the four living creatures gave to the seven angels seven golden bowls full of the wrath of God who lives forever and ever. The temple was filled with smoke from the glory of God and from His power, and no one was able to enter the temple till the seven plagues of the seven angels were completed.
>
> Revelation 15:5–8

These angels come directly from God's throne, commanded by Him. They do not act on their own authority. They are given seven golden bowls, full of the wrath of God, and they are the most severe of all the judgments so far. They are clothed in pure white linen, indicating that God's judgments are always righteous and pure. At this point, there is smoke covering the throne of God as these final judgments are handed out, and no one can enter the temple until after the plagues have been poured out. God does not take joy in handing out His judgment. He loves all His creation, even those who reject Him. It must sadden the Lord greatly when He must do what is just and righteous in dealing with those He loves. He has been patient toward all, giving everyone a chance by His great mercy. But God and evil can't dwell together. Behind the smoke, we find a saddened Father, in solemn repose, who must punish the ones He loves.

"Say to them: 'As I live,' says the Lord GOD, 'I have no pleasure in the death of the wicked, but that the wicked turn from his way and live. Turn, turn from your evil ways! For why should you die, O house of Israel?'" (Ezekiel 33:11).

The shortest verse in the Bible is John 11:35, which reads, "Jesus wept." God loves deeper than any other being. His heart feels all the emotions we would feel, only greatly magnified, for He is God. The only reason we feel love and heartache is because we were created in the image of God. We are blessed to feel emotion as He feels, even to a lesser degree. Behind the veil of smoke, we find a disheartened Father who doesn't want to be disturbed until it is over and His wrath is complete. Jesus, in His suffering and sacrifice of His life for us on the cross, took upon Himself the fullness of God's wrath. He bore our sins on His shoulders so we wouldn't have to receive God's wrath ourselves. All who are born-again will be spared from the tribulation woes, according to God's promise. We will not experience the fullness of God's wrath poured out on the world. We will not be separated from God the Father, as Jesus was. We will never have to cry to Him, "Father, why have you forsaken me?" as Jesus did on the cross. God's Word tells all believing Christians that He will never leave or forsake us.

We can trust that God, who loves His children, will keep His promises and spare us from the horrors of the tribulation. God is unwavering and always remains faithful to His promises.

> When I say to the righteous that he shall surely live, but he trusts in his own righteousness and commits iniquity, none of his righteous works shall be remembered; but because of the iniquity that he has committed, he shall die. Again, when I say to the wicked, "You shall surely die," if he turns from his sin and does what is lawful and right, if the wicked restores the pledge, gives back what he has stolen, and walks in the statutes of life without committing iniquity, he shall surely live; he shall not die. None of his sins which he has committed shall be remembered against him; he has done what is lawful and right; he shall surely live.
>
> Yet the children of your people say, "The way of the Lord is not fair." But it is their way, which is not fair!
>
> Ezekiel 33:13–17

God has given all who are in Christ the free gift of salvation, yet the wicked still reject it and shake their fists at God, wailing, "You are not fair!" But God is fair, and man condemns himself by refusing His blessing of salvation and preferring the wickedness of this world. Now, we'll move on to Revelation chapter 16, where the bowl judgments will be poured out. God's severe judgments reflect His anger toward wickedness. The world had time to repent, but now they will witness God's power and majesty.

"Then I heard a loud voice from the temple saying to the

seven angels, 'Go and pour out the bowls of the wrath of God on the earth'" (Revelation 16:1).

God commands the seven angels to go forth and begin releasing the bowl judgments. The "bowl judgments" are the most severe and dreadful of all the judgments during the tribulation. They are referred to as the "third woe" in Revelation 11:14.

"So the first went and poured out his bowl upon the earth, and a foul and loathsome sore came upon the men who had the mark of the beast and those who worshiped his image" (Revelation 16:2).

In Exodus 9:8–12, the plagues that were put upon Egypt by God through Moses are very similar to the plague given in the first bowl judgment. Just like the boils that plagued every Egyptian but spared the Israelites, these sores would only affect those who had taken the mark of the beast. Man condemns himself by continually rejecting God. So, God now marks those marked by the beast, by their own choice, with painful sores. Throughout the Bible, we have seen repeatedly that God always makes provisions to protect His people. In Exodus chapter 12, God had His people apply blood onto their doorposts to protect their firstborn children. It was the Lord's Passover. When the Lord moved that night throughout all of Egypt, striking the Egyptians' firstborn, He "passed over" all the homes that had the covering of blood upon them. He distinguished between those He needed to punish and those who were His own. In the first plague of His dispensation of justice onto the wicked, He does the same, sparing all who have refused to worship the beast and who didn't take the "mark." Just like the blood on the people's homes protected God's people from any harm as He passed over Egypt, so too will the blood of Christ protect those who love God during the tribulation.

There will not be many Christians left on the earth who

haven't been martyred at this point, but there will be some who survive and enter into the millennial kingdom. These Christians won't be affected by the plagues that those who took the mark will suffer. These bowl judgments will mirror the plagues God brought onto the Pharaoh and the Egyptians in the book of Exodus. Still, they'll be dramatically more severe, affecting earth more fiercely. Some of these plagues may seem symbolic, as we cannot envision all that is described. Still, we have no doubt these plagues will be terrifyingly real to the earth's inhabitants during the tribulation. Although the judgments during the first half of the seven-year tribulation were severe chastisements to bring repentance, these final bowl judgments will be punishments for the sole purpose of dispensing justice.

"Then the second angel poured out his bowl on the sea, and it became blood as of a dead man; and every living creature in the sea died. Then the third angel poured out his bowl on the rivers and springs of water, and they became blood" (Revelation 16:3).

The first bowl affected the earth; now, this "second bowl" affects the sea. In Revelation chapter 8, we saw a partial contamination of the sea, but here it is complete; "every living creature in the sea died." We don't know precisely how God will make this happen, but we know He is omnipotent. There is nothing He cannot do. The sea "became blood as of a dead man": Its appearance is like the blood of a dead man, but it may not be actual blood; however, it will be putrid and repulsive to humanity. The "third bowl" affects the freshwater of the earth. Like the sea, it will become wholly contaminated, making it difficult for mankind to find fresh water to drink. Humanity will be devastated in its attempt to survive. They won't be able to suffer very long under these conditions, indicating that Jesus will be returning very soon. The wickedness these antichrist followers displayed as they persecuted God's saints has brought misery and destruction upon themselves.

And I heard the angel of the waters saying: "You are righteous, O Lord, The One who is and who was and who is to be, Because You have judged these things. For they have shed the blood of saints and prophets, And You have given them blood to drink. For it is their just due." And I heard another from the altar saying, "Even so, Lord God Almighty, true and righteous are Your judgments."

Revelation 16:5–7

In these verses, we have affirmation again by the voice of the angels worshipping the Lord, proclaiming that God, the "Alpha and Omega," is righteous in judging the people of the earth. Hebrews 10:26 tells us, "For if we sin willfully after we have received the knowledge of the truth, there no longer remains a sacrifice for sins." God has given humanity at this point every opportunity to repent and turn to Christ for their salvation. Yet, humankind, in their stubborn unbelief and rejection of God, willingly chooses the world by living out their sinful lifestyles rather than repenting and accepting their Savior, Christ Jesus. They decided to believe the lie and take the mark, worshipping the antichrist rather than their Creator. God has given humanity fair warning for thousands of years, and now His wrath will be poured out upon the wicked of the world. Although it disheartens Him, justice must be served.

Then the fourth angel poured out his bowl on the sun, and power was given to him to scorch men with fire. And men were scorched with great heat, and they blasphemed the name of God who has power over these plagues; and they did not repent and give Him glory.

Revelation 16:8–9

Humanity has always enjoyed the sun's warmth; it has been a great blessing from God. People seeking recreation from their daily work have flocked to the beaches, lakes, and rivers, seeking a pleasant time of "fun in the sun" throughout the ages. God's provision of the sun has given man health benefits in absorbing vitamin D and being a necessary factor in growing produce. Trees and other plants require sunlight to sustain life. The sun has always been beneficial to humanity. But the sun will become man's common enemy here in the tribulation. When this "fourth angel" pours out his bowl on the sun, it will cause the sun to change drastically. The sun's rays will intensify dramatically, and people will no longer be able to tolerate being in the sun, even briefly. Men will be scorched with severe heat coming from the sun, and they'll be forced to hide from its rays. The nighttime will have temperatures much like the deserts during the day in the middle of summer, and the heat from the daytime sun will be unbearable.

The sun in these days will become a curse upon mankind rather than a blessing. Yet people in these last days will not learn from experience or observation; instead, they will curse and blaspheme God, who has the power to give and to take away. In the book of Job chapter 2 verse 9, Job's wife tells him to "curse God and die!" These sinners seem to have taken her advice. Rather than turning to God's mercy and forgiveness that was theirs for the asking, they chose not to repent. Man's sinful nature hinders them from responding with repentance. Yet, it was their own refusal to repent that brought these plagues down upon them. Still, if they would change their hearts, they would see God as a blessing, and God's grace, love, and mercy would anchor their salvation. John F. Walvoord wrote,

> The wishful thinking of some that men would re-
> pent if they only knew the power and righteous
> judgment of God is shattered by frequent mention

in this chapter of the hardness of the human heart in the face of the most stringent and evident divine discipline.

Humanity, in their rebellious and sinful state, often blaspheme God due to their hardened hearts and stubbornness to repent. The judgment of God does not necessarily lead to repentance. Still, the goodness of God's grace does. But man, in his free will, must choose whether or not to repent.

> Then the fifth angel poured out his bowl on the throne of the beast, and his kingdom became full of darkness; and they gnawed their tongues because of the pain. They blasphemed the God of heaven because of their pains and their sores, and did not repent of their deeds.

Revelation 16:10–11

Some see this as a symbolic darkness, but I don't believe it is. The darkness that Egypt experienced during the plague brought upon them by God, as a result of Pharaoh's hardened heart, was a physical manifestation of darkness so heavy it could be felt (Exodus chapter 10). Similarly, the darkness during the tribulation will be the same. In their unbearable pain, they would be immobilized as darkness weighed upon them like a heavy blanket, with no sensory stimulation other than the woeful cries of others in their own misery, crying out in the utter blackness around them. Jesus described the darkness of hell in Matthew 25:30: "And cast the unprofitable servant into the outer darkness. There will be weeping and gnashing of teeth." He called it the "outer darkness" in His prophetic message, describing these events in the final days. I believe this darkness here in Revelation 16:10 is a foreshadowing of the darkness of hell that these people, under the judgment of the fifth bowl, will soon experience in the "lake of fire." "They gnawed their tongues because of the pain": These sinners who went against God's people in the tribulation will be in such severe pain from all the sores and burns upon their bodies and the stings from the relentless locusts and illness from the plagues, they will be in agonizing misery by this point. Instead of crying out for God's mercy and repenting from their wickedness, they foolishly continue to curse God, the only One who could end their spiritual death. If they would turn to Christ, He would keep them from where they otherwise would be destined to spend eternity in condemnation and misery for all time.

> Then the sixth angel poured out his bowl on the great river Euphrates, and its water was dried up, so that the way of the kings from the east might be prepared. And I saw three unclean spirits like frogs coming out of the mouth of the dragon, out of the mouth of the beast, and out of the mouth of the false prophet. For they are spirits of demons, performing signs, which go out to the kings of the earth and of the whole world, to gather them to the battle of that great day of God Almighty.

> Revelation 16:12–14

In Revelation 9:14, we learn about the Euphrates as the place where four angels were kept until their release during the tribulation era. In 1 Kings chapter 22, we see a story of an angel who comes before God on his throne to lie and deceive King Ahab into battle. Satan and his fallen angels have had access to the throne of God and His ear, even today. Satan is the accuser in heaven whom Jesus, our Advocate and Intercessor at the Father's right hand, intercedes for us against Satan's accusations. This angel in 1 Kings is a fallen angel God used to deceive Ahab. The angels we saw in Revelation chapter 9, released from their bondage at the Euphrates, were fallen angels

God released for His purposes at the proper time. God can use fallen beings for His divine purpose at His discretion.

In Revelation 16:12, the Euphrates is described as "dried up." In the days of the Roman Empire, the Euphrates River was considered a barrier against any invading armies that might come from the east. The Euphrates was a vast river at that time, and there was no dam to hinder its flow. It was 1,800 miles long and between 300 and 1,200 yards wide. Many today believe if the Euphrates dried up, it would give clear access to the nations of the east, such as China, India, Pakistan, and Japan, to move against Israel. China's military is already massive in our modern times, and they, by themselves, would be a force to be reckoned with. Others believe these armies may war with the antichrist and his armies in Europe at this time, but we can only speculate as Scripture doesn't make this clear. Regardless, all nations will ultimately ally to battle God and His Messiah. Psalm chapter 2 gives prophecy to this event, declaring the Messiah's triumph and kingdom to come. Verse 13 reads, "And I saw three unclean spirits like frogs." These "frogs" are spiritual demonic entities that come forth from the mouths of Satan, the antichrist, and the false prophet to take a message to the kings of the eastern nations. They come forth from their mouths to symbolize their words, which will be used to recruit the nations against God and His Christ in war. Matthew Henry said the following:

> Hell, the secular power of antichrist, and the ecclesiastical power, would combine to send their several instruments, furnished with hellish malice, with worldly policy, and with religious falsehood and deceit; and these would muster up the devil's forces for a decisive battle.

Now, in verse 14: "For they are spirits of demons, performing signs, which go out to the kings of the earth and of the whole world, to gather them to the battle of that great day of God Almighty." These demonic spirits will convince the kings or leaders of each nation not to hesitate in making their move through deception and the false miraculous signs that come from the unholy triune. They will be convinced that joining this coalition against God will be much better than staying apart. Through deception, they will be fooled into believing they will win, and then demonically led armies will flood across the dry Euphrates, where they will soon gather with the rest of the nations in the valley at Megiddo to attack the Lord in Jerusalem.

"Behold, I am coming as a thief. Blessed is he who watches, and keeps his garments, lest he walk naked and they see his shame" (Revelation 16:15).

Jesus comes forth and makes an affirming announcement to warn and encourage all believers and followers of Christ to maintain their faith and not give up in the face of trouble. He assures them of His victory and warns His own to hold true to their faith in Him and stand firm and not be deceived by the enemy, for He (Jesus) could come at any moment. The Lord tells all who have trusted Him to hang in there a bit longer. He, just like Jesus, told His disciples not to fear man or Satan, who has no power to kill their souls, but instead fear the Lord who has that power. He encourages His followers to remain strong. In Matthew 10:28, Jesus is telling us all, "And do not fear those who kill the body but cannot kill the soul. But rather fear Him who is able to destroy both soul and body in hell." The fear of God is not like the fear you would feel if you were afraid of someone or something that frightens you. The fear of God is more of holding a reverence toward Him in awe of His power and majesty as the Sovereign Lord God Most High, who created the heavens and the earth. It is bowing down to Him alone, trusting in Him, for He is the One who gives and takes away. Our lives are sustained by the Creator, and He could end them in a moment, but He also has power over our eternal souls, which only He owns as our Creator. Thank God for His outstanding attributes of love, grace, mercy, and forgiveness, for our gracious God holds us all in His great hand. These martyrs of the tribulation, though frightened as they may be to die by the hand of the antichrist and his minions, are reminded by the Lord's assurance here that their eternal lives are much more important than their physical deaths. It will be over soon if they hold true to their faith in Him. They will find themselves in the eternal presence of their loving God rather than the eternal torment of the lake of fire by choosing the mark of the beast.

"And they gathered them together to the place called in Hebrew, Armageddon" (Revelation 16:16).

> Then the seventh angel poured out his bowl into the air, and a loud voice came out of the temple of heaven, from the throne, saying, "It is done!" And there were noises and thunderings and lightnings; and there was a great earthquake, such a mighty and great earthquake as had not occurred since men were on the earth. Now the great city was divided into three parts, and the cities of the nations fell. And great Babylon was remembered before God, to give her the cup of the wine of the fierceness of His wrath. Then every island fled away, and the mountains were not found. And great hail from heaven fell upon men, each hailstone about the weight of a talent. Men blasphemed God because of the plague of the hail, since that plague was exceedingly great.
>
> Revelation 16:17–21

Now, the seventh angel pours out the last bowl of God's wrath to punish the world. The earth will be utterly shaken, and people will try to flee, but there is nowhere safe to escape.

The seals, the trumpets, and the bowls have all been released. A loud voice from the throne said, "It is done!" God's wrath has been poured out while God has given every opportunity to the sinners left on the earth to repent and turn to Him. The judgments have been given, and now there will be no delay. The time has come for Jesus to return in glory and establish His kingdom on earth. "There were noises and thunderings and lightnings; and there was a great earthquake, such a mighty and great earthquake as had not occurred since men were on the earth." A great upheaval of the entire earth was launched when the seventh angel poured his bowl into the air. The world was convulsing under the onslaught of never-before-seen weather conditions and a great earthquake, such as had not occurred in the earth's history. Huge one-hundred-pound hailstones pummeled the earth and those upon it with ferocity. Numerous times in the Bible, God has used hailstones to bring judgment on the wicked (Exodus 9:24, Isaiah 28:2, Joshua 10:11, and Ezekiel 38:22). All these things have been experienced by humanity here on earth to a lesser degree and in localized areas of the earth; but here, the whole world was in upheaval and to a much greater degree. Not one place on the planet was without some form of cataclysmic event: islands disappearing and new mountain ranges being formed. Jesus spoke of this in His Olivet Discourse:

> Immediately after the tribulation of those days the sun will be darkened, and the moon will not give its light; the stars will fall from heaven, and the powers of the heavens will be shaken. Then the sign of the Son of Man will appear in heaven, and then all the tribes of the earth will mourn, and they will see the Son of Man coming on the clouds of heaven with power and great glory.
>
> Matthew 24:29–30

Man has never before seen such turmoil and upheaval upon the earth. But it wasn't over yet.

CHAPTER 9

THE FALL OF BABYLON

Jesus was coming again to the earth, and all would see Him, the Son of Man, coming on clouds and with great glory. The nations of the world would soon be mourning. These nations and their leaders were astonished by what was taking place on the earth and desperate to find a way to defeat the coming Lord. Matthew Henry writes,

> The fall of Babylon, which was divided into three parts, called the cities of the nations (Revelation 16:19); having had rule over the nations, and taken in the idolatry of the nations, incorporating into her religion something of the Jewish, something of the pagan, and something of the Christian religion, she was as three cities in one. God now remembered this great and wicked city. Though for some time he seemed to have forgotten her idolatry and cruelty, yet now he gives unto her the cup of the wine of the fierceness of his wrath. And this downfall extended further than to the seat of antichrist; it reached from the centre to the circumference; and every island and every mountain, that seemed by nature and situation the most secured, were carried away in the deluge of this ruin.

In utter depravity and unrepentance, the nations in the

grip of spiritual Babylon plotted their war schemes against God. Satan knew those who dwell on the earth were ripe for the picking. He and his wicked horde quickly hurried to deceive them into believing they could come up against the returning Lord with enough power to win. In chapters 17 and 18 of Revelation, we will get into more detail about the fall of Babylon. Still, here we see that their downfall is already beginning. Babylon will soon drink from the cup of the fierceness of God's wrath. A prophetic picture of the turmoil of the earth in this time of judgment was given by God to Isaiah thousands of years ago. Isaiah 24:17–18 reads,

> Fear and the pit and the snare Are upon you, O inhabitant of the earth. And it shall be That he who flees from the noise of the fear Shall fall into the pit, And he who comes up from the midst of the pit Shall be caught in the snare; For the windows from on high are open, And the foundations of the earth are shaken.

The kings of the earth are falling into the finality of their judgment as they try to find a way to escape it. But you can't escape God's judgment; the only way to stop it is by satisfying God, and the only way to satisfy God can only be found in Christ on the cross. Matthew Henry wrote,

> How the antichristian party were affected with it. Though it fell upon them as a dreadful storm, as if the stones of the city, tossed up into the air, came down upon their heads, like hailstones of a talent weight each, yet they were so far from repenting that they blasphemed that God who thus punished them. Here was a dreadful plague of the heart, a spiritual judgment more dreadful and destructive than all the rest. Observe,

1. The greatest calamities that can befall men will not bring them to repentance without the grace of God working with them.

2. Those that are not made better by the judgments of God are always the worse for them.

3. To be hardened in sin and enmity against God by his righteous judgments is a certain token of utter destruction. But these depraved leaders refuse to repent.

Soon, these kings of Babylon will know the power and glory of the Lord of lords and King of kings. The Lord "will punish on high the host of exalted ones, And on the earth the kings of the earth" (Isaiah 24:21), and the Lord of Hosts will reign in Jerusalem!

The earth shall reel to and fro like a drunkard, And shall totter like a hut; Its transgression shall be heavy upon it, And it will fall, and not rise again.

It shall come to pass in that day That the LORD will punish on high the host of exalted ones, And on the earth the kings of the earth. They will be gathered together, As prisoners are gathered in the pit, And will be shut up in the prison; After many days they will be punished. Then the moon will be disgraced And the sun ashamed; For the LORD of hosts will reign On Mount Zion and in Jerusalem And before His elders, gloriously.

Isaiah 24:20–23

As we move into chapters 17 and 18 of Revelation, we will gain further insight into the fall of Babylon:

Then one of the seven angels who had the seven bowls came and talked with me, saying to me, "Come, I will show you the judgment of the great harlot who sits on many waters, with whom the kings of the earth committed fornication, and the inhabitants of the earth were made drunk with the wine of her fornication."

Revelation 17:1–2

Here, we see the specific judgment of God upon the false religious system, Babylon, that great spiritual harlot who has tempted humanity and sent so many to hell through the ages by the use of lies and deception. "I will show you the judgment of the great harlot who sits on many waters": The "harlot" (or "whore', used in the KJV) is the false church system that was very powerful and ruled over many nations. This false church system will help the beast to gain power. "Many waters" refers to the "nations" influenced by the system. In Matthew 7:15, we are told by Jesus in His sermon on the mount: "Beware of false prophets, who come to you in sheep's clothing, but inwardly they are ravenous wolves." The "ravenous wolves" are the false church systems that have risen over the centuries. Their false teachings have kept many from the truth of the gospel for hundreds of years. Pagan beliefs in Babylon society intermingled with Christian beliefs, bringing carnality into the temples and leading people astray, corrupting them in sin. They introduced carnality as a form of worship. These were an abomination to God.

We first saw Babylon in chapter 11 of Genesis. Still, after God saw that the people were one and had one common language, He came down from heaven. He confused their language and scattered them because of their pride in making a name for themselves. God saw that if he didn't scatter them and slow their progress, "nothing that they propose to do will be withheld from them" (Genesis 11:4–9). Babylon, the city, after the building of the tower was stopped, came to be known spiritually as any nation that turned its backs on God and reveled in spiritual ruin, committing idolatry and spiritual fornication. As time went on, the essence of Babylon became a "false religious system" that led men to trust in something other than Jesus Christ for their salvation. They promoted salvation by works rather than trusting in God's grace alone through Jesus Christ. This was contrary to what the Bible itself teaches. By following these false systems of religious doctrine, man, in their pursuit of godliness, strayed back to the concept of Babel, believing that by their own efforts, they could work their way into heaven. Pastor Chuck Smith wrote,

> Babylon is used in the scripture as a symbol of con-fusion, because it was in Babylon where man, in rebellion against the living God, decided to build a tower whereby they could communicate with the universe. Ancient man was not as primitive and ig-norant as we think him to be. They had tremendous means of communication. Perhaps even superior to ours, because there are indications that they had de-veloped methods whereby they could communicate with other beings outside of the earth.

The "tower" that the Babylonians were building seemed in their minds a means to get to heaven on their own, without any need for God. God came down and confused their language to separate them from each other. Humankind tried to reach for the heavens themselves rather than receiving salvation by God's provision. It is man's nature to attempt to get to heaven by their own works rather than God's grace. All religions today, besides Christianity, are based on a works system designed to achieve salvation. Nimrod, the king of Babylon, was a fore-shadowing of the spirit of the antichrist. His wife Semiramis, an "idol-worshipping priestess," started the Babylonian religion in the city of Babylon that would later become the spiritual essence of the false religious systems that would rise in the world, known as "Mystery Babylon." It would apply to any religious system that would turn away from the gospel message of salvation by grace alone, authentic Christianity. Many evil conquerors and dictators throughout history have displayed this spirit. Ahab, Alexander, Hitler, Stalin, and Mao Tse-tung were all wicked leaders functioning under the spirit of the antichrist, to name a few. The Israelite king, Ahab, and his wife, Jezebel, were two of the most evil characters in the Bible. Ahab "set up an altar for Baal in the temple of Baal, which he had built in Samaria. And Ahab made a wooden image. Ahab did more to provoke the LORD God of Israel to anger than all the kings of Israel who were before him" (1 Kings 16:32–33). And Jezebel "massacred the prophets of the LORD" (1 Kings 18:4). The Babylonian religious system came into being long before Christ died on the cross and Christianity was born. "And I saw a woman sitting on a scarlet beast which was full of names of blasphemy, having seven heads and ten horns" (Revelation 17:3). In Genesis 11:1–10, we see Babylon (Babel, meaning "confusion") as a literal city on the Euphrates River. Professor Merrill C. Tenney, in his writing about Babylon, stated,

> [It] was the seat of the civilization that expressed organized hostility to God. Babylon was later the capital of the empire that cruelly conquered Judah. Babylon, to them (the Jews), was the essence of all evil, the embodiment of cruelty, the foe of God's people, and the lasting type of sin, carnality, lust and greed.

Since the days of the actual city of Babylon, man has falsely believed he could devise a better plan to reach heaven. As man has sought to create their own religious system, they have created confusion within the church and a false religious system as a way to reach God and His kingdom. They have established a system in which certain individuals in the church, namely the clergy, are considered more righteous than others. Men in certain positions become a type of mediator who will function as God's representative on earth. Still, in our communion with Christ, they are no different than you or me. They are, according to their belief, which is not based on the truth of God's Word, a kind of "middleman" between you and God. You confess your sins to them instead of to God in prayer. They falsely present themselves as God's established representative. This makes them appear more righteous than any other "born-again" believer not part of the clergy. They intercede for you, then give you absolution, telling you, "You're forgiven." But no man can forgive sin, only God. This is undoubtedly false teaching because, as we are told in 1 Timothy 2:5, "For there is one God and one Mediator between God and men, the Man Christ Jesus." This is the product of someone distorting God's Word by blending it with their own ideas. The Jehovah's Witnesses and Mormonists do this as well.

For many years, the ordinary person had no access to a translation of the Holy Bible that they could read for themselves. Hence, they had to rely on the "honesty" of the clergy to translate its meaning for them. People completely trusted in man rather than the truth of God, and they believed everything these "middlemen" told them was true.

Martin Luther fought against these things against the Catholic church when Protestantism was formed. He translated the Bible from Latin to German so the commoner could read it. He taught that salvation and eternal life were not earned by "good deeds" but by a person's faith in Jesus Christ, a free gift of God's grace. This led to Him falling into disfavor with the pope and being condemned as an outlaw by the Holy Roman Emperor.

The false religious systems used deception and false teaching to steer humanity from the truth throughout the ages. Millions of people have been fooled into forming false religious beliefs and adhering to them all their lives in all parts of the world today. It was by the influence of Satan, in the spirit of Mystery Babylon. The truth is, they are not any more righteous than you as a follower of Christ, and you are not any more righteous than them.

God looks at all true believers in Christ the same way. He doesn't see any person as being more righteous or holier than someone else. He sees us as He sees His only Son. As Christians, we are justified and righteous in His sight because of our trust and faith in Jesus Christ and His work on the cross. Jesus established His church as perfect, then after two decades, man became involved and added his own beliefs, rules, and systems, which brought confusion. This created dissent within the religious churches, and people began competing for power, position, and authority. Those in higher positions within the church started misusing their authority and "ruling" over others because of the Adamic nature of humankind. This is not what Jesus wanted. We see this in Mark 10:42–45:

> But Jesus called them to Himself and said to them, "You know that those who are considered rulers over the Gentiles lord it over them, and their great ones exercise authority over them. Yet it shall not be so among you; but whoever desires to become great among you shall be your servant. And whoever of you desires to be first shall be slave of all. For even the Son of Man did not come to be served, but to serve, and to give His life a ransom for many."

Men brought confusion into the apostate religions that have developed throughout the church age to become the worldwide and powerful organized assembly they have established around the globe today. The organized religious churches in the past became so powerful that they ruled over kings and nations. But as we see here, during the tribulation described in Revelation chapter 17, God is about to bring certain judgment upon these false religious systems that have confused humanity and turned them away from the truth of God's Word. Spiritual Babylon is about to fall.

> So he carried me away in the Spirit into the wilderness. And I saw a woman sitting on a scarlet beast which was full of names of blasphemy, having seven heads and ten horns. The woman was arrayed in purple and scarlet, and adorned with gold and precious stones and pearls, having in her hand a golden cup full of abominations and the filthiness of her fornication. And on her forehead a name was written:
>
> MYSTERY, BABYLON THE GREAT, THE MOTHER OF HARLOTS AND OF THE ABOMINATIONS OF THE EARTH.
>
> I saw the woman, drunk with the blood of the saints and with the blood of the martyrs of Jesus. And when I saw her, I marveled with great amazement.
>
> Revelation 17:3–6

John was taken in the Spirit into the wilderness, where he was presented with this vision of a woman riding a beast. The image is so profound that he is astonished by the sight of her sitting upon this "scarlet beast" mentioned in the verse. John F. Walvoord writes, "Her position, that of riding the beast, indicates on the one hand that she is supported by the political power of the beast, and on the other that she is in a dominant role and at least outwardly controls and directs the beast."

John sees the woman drunk with the blood of the saints and the martyrs, which indicates she not only revels in their deaths but has a part in their executions. On her forehead is the name, "Mystery Babylon, Mother of Harlots and the Abominations of the Earth," denoting her as the one responsible for the spiritual fornication and idolatry that began in the world religions. Babylon is referred to here as "Mystery Babylon," which tells us the woman doesn't represent the actual city of Babylon but something that spiritually personifies Babylon. The city is typically used to represent the world's religious domain and political and economic facets. When the true church is raptured just before the tribulation, the apostate church will rise and take its place. This "false religion" of spiritual Babylon will begin to persecute those who have placed their trust in Jesus Christ. This religion won't preach the gospel, Christ's death, burial, and resurrection, nor His return to earth at the second coming. Instead, it will promote ritual rather than revival, focusing on prosperity and bettering oneself rather than spiritual truth for salvation. Out of the apostate religions, the false prophet will be produced onto the world stage. He will join with and exalt the antichrist. "And I saw a woman sitting on a scarlet beast which was full of names of blasphemy, having seven heads and ten horns." The "beast" is the same beast we saw in chapters 12 and 13, representing the antichrist. The seven heads and ten horns represent his dictatorship, the coalition or federation of nations that are his. "The woman was arrayed in purple and scarlet, and adorned with gold and precious stones and pearls, having in her hand a golden cup full of abominations and the filthiness of her fornication": This represents the cup that the organized and powerful religions have drank from throughout the centuries. They are the Laodicean church and have deceived and manipulated humanity for personal gain, using a false religion to benefit themselves, for many centuries. To the people of the earth, the woman of Mystery Babylon appears quite religious, having the "faith" everybody desires. Donald Grey Barnhouse, a noted Theologian and Pastor, wrote, "We find in the course of church history that one of the deadliest marks of ecclesiastical corruption is the lust for temporal power."

As for the verse, "The woman was arrayed in purple and scarlet, and adorned with gold and precious stones and pearls," the dyes required to make purple and scarlet fabric were very costly. These colors usually denoted a political or economic leader with authority. They were the colors of kings and high-ranking officials. Interestingly, the bishops and the papacy within the Vatican church in Rome often wear "purple and scarlet" robes. The Vatican, the headquarters of the organized Catholic church, is a government to itself, acquiring great wealth over the centuries. It could be the world's most prosperous government or religious entity. No one but the Vatican knows how much wealth they have obtained over the centuries, for they are self-regulated and governed.

Although Catholicism doesn't compare to the early carnal and pagan religious practices of the false temples in the ancient city of Babylon, they do teach non-biblical, man-constructed rules, rituals, and ideas. The Holy Bible was banned from anyone not part of the clergy when the early Catholic church began. Some Bible scholars believe the false prophet may arise from the papacy, but this is speculation. There is no scriptural basis for believing this to be the case. I don't mean to single out the Catholic church here, but they are the closest example that is commonly known today that I can refer to. It is the largest organized church in the world today. However, they do seem to mirror these types of religious organizations, as described in these chapters of Revelation: those who do not adhere to the Scriptures and add to the Bible teachings. Any church that introduces its own ideas and doctrine that does not adhere to the Bible's teachings can be considered an apostate church teaching apostasy. "Mormonism" and "Jehovah's Witnesses" are other examples of these kinds of churches. However, it is up to the student of Scripture to understand the truth for themselves through discernment with the help of the Holy Spirit. Some of the most heinous acts were done throughout history in the name of "Christianity." Still, these actions done in the name of the Lord had nothing to do with genuine Christian beliefs.

The Crusades, the Inquisition, and the Dark Ages are three well-known times in history when religion ruled over the actions of men, and true Christians were severely persecuted. Under the reign of Queen Mary of England, who was known as "Bloody Mary," hundreds of Christians were burned at the stake in the name of Catholicism. Whether the Catholic church or the pope will be relevant to these end-times events during the tribulation can only be speculated. No one will know for sure until it is revealed in the time established by God for this to take place in this world. But we, members of the body of Christ, will not experience these things. We will not be here during the tribulation, for we will be with our Lord in heaven, experiencing the marriage of the Lamb and the marriage supper of the Lamb. We will be busy in heaven, preparing to return to earth, following our Lord and King Jesus to begin His rule and reign. Now John hears from the angel, who explains these things he has seen:

> But the angel said to me, "Why did you marvel? I will tell you the mystery of the woman and of the beast that carries her, which has the seven heads and the ten horns. The beast that you saw was, and is not, and will ascend out of the bottomless pit and go to perdition. And those who dwell on the

earth will marvel, whose names are not written in the Book of Life from the foundation of the world, when they see the beast that was, and is not, and yet is.

"Here is the mind which has wisdom: The seven heads are seven mountains on which the woman sits. There are also seven kings. Five have fallen, one is, and the other has not yet come. And when he comes, he must continue a short time. The beast that was, and is not, is himself also the eighth, and is of the seven, and is going to perdition.

"The ten horns which you saw are ten kings who have received no kingdom as yet, but they receive authority for one hour as kings with the beast. These are of one mind, and they will give their power and authority to the beast."

Revelation 17:7–13

"The beast that you saw was, and is not, and will ascend out of the bottomless pit and go to perdition." So, we know "the beast" is the antichrist possessed by Satan. The angel reveals to John, "Here is the mind which has wisdom: The seven heads are seven mountains on which the woman sits." Many scholars believe the "seven mountains" are Rome, but some do not. Rome is known as the city of seven hills. These scholars who do not think it's Rome claim that the Greek word here describes "mountains" and not "hills." In either case, we know a revised Roman Empire will rise after the fall of the Roman Empire that was powerful during the days Jesus walked the earth. However, it will not be as strong as the first one because it will consist of ten smaller nations. In Daniel's prophetic explanation about Nebuchadnezzar's dream, the head of the statue, being gold, represented the Babylonian Empire under the rule of King Nebuchadnezzar. This was the first powerful world-dominating empire. The second empire, the statue of arms and chest of silver, represents the Medo-Persian Empire that replaced Babylon. Then, the third empire to come, the bronze midsection of the statue representing the Greek Empire under Alexander. Then, the fourth, the legs of iron, is the ancient Roman Empire. Now, we come to the feet and toes, which in our present time is an empire that has yet to rise. It is represented as a mixture of iron and clay (Daniel 2:31–45). Iron represents the strength of the old Roman Empire, mingled with clay, denoting they are weaker because this empire of the tribulation will be comprised not of one strong nation but of many nations with ten kings who will answer to their king, the antichrist. This means they are not kings but receive the same kind of power as a king. Their leader will be the antichrist himself. These kings are represented by the toes of Nebuchadnezzar's dream statue that we see in Daniel chapter 2; they are the federation of kings who will answer to the antichrist. These ten kings of the ten-nation European coalition under the dictatorship of the antichrist will be formed in the days that the Lord will set up His kingdom according to Daniel 2:44. In the verse, we see: "In the days of these kings the God of heaven will set up a kingdom which shall never be destroyed," referring to the coming rule and reign of Jesus on earth. Some Bible scholars believe these kings to be the "revised Roman Empire" that will rise during the end times, in the days of the antichrist, that Jesus will bash into pieces upon His return to establish His kingdom. So, Daniel's prophecy declares that the coming of Christ will take place during the time of the rule of these ten kings of the European community, in the time of the great tribulation. "The ten horns which you saw are ten kings who have received no kingdom as yet, but they receive authority for one hour as kings with the beast. These are of one mind, and they will give their power and authority to the beast" (Revelation 17:12–13).

These ten kings have given their power to the "beast" so that through their combined efforts, they might destroy the Lord and His kingdom, making war against Him as He returns. Their combined efforts are to try and stop the establishment of God's law and God's rule upon the earth. It is a last-ditch effort to keep God from ruling. Theologian Henry Alford wrote,

> They are ten kingdoms which shall arise out of the fourth great kingdom there: ten European powers, which in the last time, in concert with and subjugation to the antichristian power, shall make war against Christ. In the precise number and form here indicated, they have not yet arisen…What changes in Europe may bring them into the required tale and form, it is not for us to say.

"Mystery Babylon," the religious system that has permeated the earth and led many souls to their doom, is about to be dealt with by the political power that previously supported her and ultimately by the Living God Most High. During the great tribulation, God calls all believers to stand firm in their faith and not compromise. Though this worldwide religious and economic system may appear "all-powerful," it is not. Help is on the way. God will soon deal with Babylon in a sudden act of His power, so salvation for the saints is near. He encourages all believers not to follow the "mob" of people who have been deceived by the antichrist. Many individuals have been swayed by groupthink, or "mob mentality," even in modern times. Still, there will be strong delusion in these last days of the tribulation. People will be desperate and cling to what seems to them the perfect solution to their problems. God is in control, His will be done on earth as it is in heaven, and He will soon make everything right, but first, this spiritually wicked and false religious system will succumb to the attack of the federation of nations led by the antichrist who will turn on her. Where once she was an ally, now she is hated by the antichrist and his dictatorship. Some Bible scholars have seen the "European Union" that exists today as the potential fulfillment of this future coalition of nations. However, more than ten nations are in this revived European power, and more are on the way. By their own admission, the Union claims to be a successor to the ancient Roman Empire. Six European nations met to discuss combining fuel and economic resources in 1957. They met in Rome and signed the "Treaty of Rome," which began the present European Union. The European Union flag is as conspicuous as any national flag throughout Europe. Could this be the start of the revised Roman Empire under the dictatorship of the coming antichrist? Only time will tell. Now here, during the tribulation, these kings of ten nations are destined to face the Lord of lords in battle, and when they do, it will be over before they know what hit them.

"These will make war with the Lamb, and the Lamb will overcome them, for He is Lord of lords and King of kings; and those who are with Him are called, chosen, and faithful."

Then he said to me, "The waters which you saw, where the harlot sits, are peoples, multitudes, nations, and tongues. And the ten horns which you saw on the beast, these will hate the harlot, make her desolate and naked, eat her flesh and burn her with fire. For God has put it into their hearts to fulfill His purpose, to be of one mind, and to give their kingdom to the beast, until the words of God are fulfilled. And the woman whom you saw is that great city which reigns over the kings of the earth."

Revelation 17:14–18

In Matthew Henry's commentary on these verses, he writes as follows:

> Here is a war begun between the beast and his followers, and the Lamb and his followers. The beast and his army, to an eye of sense, appear much stronger than the Lamb and his army: one would think an army with a lamb at the head of them could not stand before the great red dragon. But, Here is a victory gained by the Lamb: The Lamb shall overcome. Christ must reign till all enemies be put under his feet; he will be sure to meet with many enemies, and much opposition, but he will also be sure to gain the victory. Here is the ground or reason of the victory assigned; and this is taken, From the character of the Lamb: He is King of kings and Lord of lords. He has, both by nature and by office, supreme dominion and power over all things; all the powers of earth and hell are subject to his check and control. From the character of his followers: They are called, and chosen, and faithful. They are called out by commission to this warfare; they are chosen and fitted for it, and they will be faithful in it. Such an army, under such a commander, will at length carry all the world before them. The victory is justly aggrandized. By the vast multitude who paid obedience and subjection to the beast and to the whore. She sat upon (that is, presided over) many waters; and these waters were so many multitudes of peo-

ple, and nations, of all languages; yea, she reigned not only over kingdoms, but over the kings, and they were her tributaries and vassals, v. 15, 18. By the powerful influence which God hereby showed he had over the minds of great men. Their hearts were in his hand, and he turned them as he pleased; for, It was of God, and to fulfil his will, that these kings agreed to give their kingdom unto the beast; they were judicially blinded and hardened to do so. And, It was of God that afterwards their hearts were turned against the whore, to hate her, and to make her desolate and naked, and to eat her flesh, and burn her with fire; they shall at length see their folly, and how they have been bewitched and enslaved by the papacy, and, out of a just resentment, shall not only fall off from Rome, but shall be made the instruments of God's providence in her destruction.

The next chapter of Revelation will conclude the fall of Mystery Babylon. But like the religious Mystery Babylon was symbolic of all false religions, there is also a commercial side to spiritual Babylon, and it will be symbolic of all the great economies and authoritarian governments of the world. God will end the corruption and deceit used to influence humanity over thousands of years, politically and commercially. Chapter 17 deals with the downfall of the religious "Mystery Babylon." Chapter 18 deals with the destruction of commercial Babylon, the great cities, governments, and merchants that have deceitfully lorded over humanity for their personal gain of power and wealth. Babylon is a satanically introduced spirit that has been turning mankind away from God and oppressing the saints for too long. Between the prophecies of chapter 17 and chapter 18, there is a gap between the two of three-and-a-half years. The prophecy of Mystery Babylon foretells their fall at the midpoint of the tribulation, and the fall of commercial Babylon will be at the end of the tribulation, just before Jesus is about to return to the earth. John F. Walvoord said the following in his commentary on these scriptures:

> The destruction of Babylon in chapter 18 should be compared with the preceding announcement in 16:19 where the great city is divided and the cities of the Gentiles fall. This event comes late in the great tribulation, just prior to the second coming of Christ, in contrast to the destruction of the harlot of chapter 17 which seems to precede the great tribulation and paves the way for the worship of the beast (Revelation 13:8).

Now, as we move into chapter 18, John sees another angel coming down from heaven whose glory illuminates the earth.

> After these things I saw another angel coming down from heaven, having great authority, and the earth was illuminated with his glory. And he cried mightily with a loud voice, saying, "Babylon the great is fallen, is fallen, and has become a dwelling place of demons, a prison for every foul spirit, and a cage for every unclean and hated bird! For all the nations have drunk of the wine of the wrath of her fornication, the kings of the earth have committed fornication with her, and the merchants of the earth have become rich through the abundance of her luxury."
>
> And I heard another voice from heaven saying, "Come out of her, my people, lest you share in her sins, and lest you receive of her plagues. For her sins

have reached to heaven, and God has remembered her iniquities. Render to her just as she rendered to you, and repay her double according to her works; in the cup which she has mixed, mix double for her. In the measure that she glorified herself and lived luxuriously, in the same measure give her torment and sorrow; for she says in her heart, 'I sit as queen, and am no widow, and will not see sorrow.' Therefore her plagues will come in one day—death and mourning and famine. And she will be utterly burned with fire, for strong is the Lord God who judges her."

Revelation 18:1–8

The angel messenger from God emphatically shouts out twice that Babylon has fallen! It "has become a dwelling place of demons;" this world during the tribulation is about to change drastically for all the nations that knew her, drank of her, and enriched themselves because of her, and now she has fallen. The spirit of greed and the lust for power has been conceived and birthed upon the earth since man first thought he did not need God and could transcend by his own capabilities. This is the spirit of Babylon in the world, and it was initiated by the influence of Satan on humanity. Whether it is the religious Mystery Babylon or it is a commercial/political Babylon, the spirit is the same and an abomination to God. John hears another voice come out of heaven, saying, "Come out of her, my people, lest you share in her sins, and lest you receive of her plagues." Just as Lot was warned not to stay amid great sin which was taking place in Sodom to avoid receiving the same punishment for their sins, this too was a warning to the saints not to give in to the temptations of this worldly system of Babylon. The materialistic enticements of the world have led man away from God throughout the ages. Since Cain first killed Abel, man has murdered, robbed, and deceived other men for their own personal gain. It is the sinful Adamic nature of man since the fall, which is responsible because humanity had chosen to believe Satan's lies over God's truth. But now God will soon make all things right again upon the earth through the One who bore humanity's sins on the cross.

The call to depart from the worldliness of Babylon has been echoed throughout the Scriptures in both the Old and the New Testament. In Isaiah 52:11, we see, "Depart! Depart! Go out from there, Touch no unclean thing; Go out from the midst of her, Be clean, You who bear the vessels of the LORD." And in Jeremiah 51:45: "My people, go out of the midst of her! And let everyone deliver himself from the fierce anger of the LORD." In 2 Kings 10:31, another heed is given, "But Jehu took no heed to walk in the law of the LORD God of Israel with all his heart; for he did not depart from the sins of Jeroboam, who had made Israel sin."

Many, sadly, will not heed the Lord's warnings; they will ignore the Word of God and count it as foolishness. They mock and laugh at God and all those who are believers. They ask, "Where is God?" "Where is the Lord's return?" During this time of trouble, they will foolishly believe they are too wise to believe in a living God. They'll consider themselves good and decent people who need nothing but themselves and their own "moral compass" to survive. This is the nature of man; God calls everyone to Himself, but many don't heed the call. When a man doesn't recognize his own sin, he is lost. God, in His great mercy and long-suffering patience, will give man every opportunity to turn away from the pursuit of evil and repent and turn to Him, but eventually, there will come a time when He can wait no longer, and judgment will come. Paul told us, "Do not be unequally yoked together with unbelievers. For what fellowship has righteousness with lawlessness? And what communion has light with darkness?" (2 Corinthians 6:14).

In this time during the tribulation, the satanic system known as Babylon will be a city immersed in evil affairs and transgressions against God. Since Babylon is a spirit that can be instilled in any city, this could be any city where the antichrist holds office. In our modern world today, Los Angeles could be called "Babylon" or any city that has given itself to wanton behavior and the corrupt pursuit of money and pleasure. During the tribulation, Babylon will be the city where world banking and commercial interests are centered. It could even be Jerusalem itself, for during this time, it becomes trodden by the Gentiles. In Revelation 11:8, we see Jerusalem referred to as: "the great city which spiritually is called Sodom and Egypt, where also our Lord was crucified," speaking about the place where the dead bodies of the "two witnesses" will be displayed for three-and-a-half-days. The description in verse 11:8 clearly shows it is Jerusalem, and it is, according to this verse, considered a place of satanic occupation. Chapter 18 references Babylon without specifying a particular city. This city in our time doesn't exist yet. It may be built during the tribulation by the antichrist as his "capital city" and the center of all his economic and commercial interests.

> For her sins have reached to heaven, and God has remembered her iniquities. Render to her just as she rendered to you, and repay her double according to her works; in the cup which she has mixed, mix double for her. In the measure that she glorified herself and lived luxuriously, in the same measure give her torment and sorrow.

Revelation 18:5–7

Our God of the New Testament is the same God of the Old Testament. He is the God of Abraham, Isaac, and Jacob. He is the God who became flesh and sacrificed Himself on the cross to save the world. Our God is unchanging. He is the same yesterday, today, and tomorrow. Our Lord, Jesus, refers to Himself as the Beginning and the End, and He has always existed and will always exist. God is always in control and has judged mankind since the beginning of man's creation. So, we see here in Revelation 18:5–8 the same kind of justice as we find in the Old Testament:

"Eye for eye, tooth for tooth, hand for hand, foot for foot" (Exodus 21:24).

"Fracture for fracture, eye for eye, tooth for tooth; as he has caused disfigurement of a man, so shall it be done to him" (Leviticus 24:20).

"Your eye shall not pity: life shall be for life, eye for eye, tooth for tooth, hand for hand, foot for foot" (Deuteronomy 19:21).

Babylon, the sinful essence of the wickedness in the world, who has grown rich in luxury, wealth, and commercial prosperity, will be destroyed. Like Sodom and Gomorrah of the Old Testament, she will be utterly burned with fire in just one day by the Almighty God.

> The kings of the earth who committed fornication
> and lived luxuriously with her will weep and lament
> for her, when they see the smoke of her burning,
> standing at a distance for fear of her torment, say-
> ing, "Alas, alas, that great city Babylon, that mighty
> city! For in one hour your judgment has come."
>
> Revelation 18:9–10

Given the current direction of governments in our modern world, it seems like this verse describes a nuclear detonation. The fact that it happens in "one hour" implies the explosion of a nuclear blast. It says the "kings of the earth…weep and lament…standing at a distance for fear of her torment." The radiation that is a result of such a blast would cause torment to those who would go near, and fear would keep many leaders of the nations from getting too close. "The smoke of her burning" could be the mushroom cloud and smoke that would linger from this type of explosion. These kings of the antichrist will not realize their wickedness and repent, even in the face of this cataclysmic event, nor will they believe that God has caused this. They will remain blind to the truth, blanketed with strong delusion in these final days until their demise.

> And the merchants of the earth will weep and mourn over her, for no one buys their merchandise anymore: merchandise of gold and silver, precious stones and pearls, fine linen and purple, silk and scarlet, every kind of citron wood, every kind of object of ivory, every kind of object of most precious wood, bronze, iron, and marble; and cinnamon and incense, fragrant oil and frankincense, wine and oil, fine flour and wheat, cattle and sheep, horses and chariots, and bodies and souls of men. The fruit that your soul longed for has gone from you, and all the things which are rich and splendid have gone from you, and you shall find them no more at all. The merchants of these things, who became rich by her, will stand at a distance for fear of her torment, weeping and wailing, and saying, "Alas, alas, that great city that was clothed in fine linen, purple, and scarlet, and adorned with gold and precious stones and pearls! For in one hour such great riches came to nothing." Every shipmaster, all who travel by ship, sailors, and as many as trade on the sea, stood at a

distance and cried out when they saw the smoke of her burning, saying, "What is like this great city?"

They threw dust on their heads and cried out, weeping and wailing, and saying, "Alas, alas, that great city, in which all who had ships on the sea became rich by her wealth! For in one hour she is made desolate."

Rejoice over her, O heaven, and you holy apostles and prophets, for God has avenged you on her!

Revelation 18:11–20

All those who bathed in the city's riches now mourn along with the kings. All the people who have gained wealth from the prosperity of the antichrist's leadership have lost all in just one moment. There is nothing left; they are all ruined. No more sumptuous dinners, extravagant and expensive jewelry, yachts, and cars. No more indulgence in the finest this world has to offer. The social elites and celebrities will no longer be parading pridefully in their wealth, wearing luxurious designer clothing and jewelry at events designed to accentuate their vanities. All those who gained wealth exploiting others will lament and mourn. They will curse and blaspheme God right up until the moment they are destroyed. Babylon is finished, and Jesus will be on His way soon to take back what is His and reign on the earth with His saints.

Then a mighty angel took up a stone like a great millstone and threw it into the sea, saying, "Thus with violence the great city Babylon shall be thrown down, and shall not be found anymore. The sound of harpists, musicians, flutists, and trumpeters shall not be heard in you anymore. No craftsman of any craft shall be found in you anymore, and the sound of a millstone shall not be heard in you anymore. The light of a lamp shall not shine in you anymore, and the voice of bridegroom and bride shall not be heard in you anymore. For your merchants were the great men of the earth, for by your sorcery all the nations were deceived. And in her was found the blood of prophets and saints, and of all who were slain on the earth."

Revelation 18:21–24

This "millstone" the angel throws into the sea brings other verses of the Bible to mind. In Jeremiah 51:60–64, we see the following:

> So Jeremiah wrote in a book all the evil that would come upon Babylon, all these words that are written against Babylon. And Jeremiah said to Seraiah, "When you arrive in Babylon and see it, and read all these words, then you shall say, 'O Lord, You have spoken against this place to cut it off, so that none shall remain in it, neither man nor beast, but it shall be desolate forever.' Now it shall be, when you have finished reading this book, that you shall tie a stone to it and throw it out into the Euphrates. Then you shall say, 'Thus Babylon shall sink and not rise from the catastrophe that I will bring upon her. And they shall be weary.'"

Thus far are the words of Jeremiah.

This scripture foretells the fall of Babylon that we've seen here in chapters 17 and 18. This coastal city may sink into the ocean and be forgotten forever when the angel casts his stone. But it is not certain. We also read in Matthew 18:6 the words of Jesus: "But whoever causes one of these little ones who believe in Me to sin, it would be better for him if a millstone were hung around his neck, and he were drowned in the depth of the sea." Babylon had led others into sin, and Jesus' words apply here to Babylon in chapter 18. Sin is bad enough when we commit it ourselves, but causing others to sin by our sinfulness is far worse. In Revelation chapter 18, we saw God's judgment on the Babylonian systems that have lured humanity into sin. In the next chapter, we will see our Lord, Jesus Christ, returning in His glory!

CHAPTER 10

THE KING RETURNS

After these things I heard a loud voice of a great multitude in heaven, saying, "Alleluia! Salvation and glory and honor and power belong to the Lord our God! For true and righteous are His judgments, because He has judged the great harlot who corrupted the earth with her fornication; and He has avenged on her the blood of His servants shed by her." Again they said, "Alleluia! Her smoke rises up forever and ever!" And the twenty-four elders and the four living creatures fell down and worshiped God who sat on the throne, saying, "Amen! Alleluia!"

Revelation 19:1–4

Shouts of praise ring out in heaven, for God's judgments have been poured out, and that great spiritual harlot of Babylon has been defeated; she is dead. She will never lead anyone astray or persecute and murder God's people again. A great multitude of heavenly beings to raise their voices in cheer, saying, "Alleluia! Salvation and glory and honor and power belong to the Lord our God!" in praise and worship of the God Most High! He has avenged the blood of His servants shed by the harlot who thought herself too great and powerful to ever be defeated. God's judgment has fallen upon the harlot of Babylon, who corrupted the earth with her fornication. The twenty-four elders fell down with the four living creatures and worshipped God on the throne, saying, "Amen, Alleluia!" Soon, the vast army that has gathered together near Megiddo, along with Satan, the antichrist, and the false prophet, will attack the Lord and His armies in a futile attempt to overpower Him. The unholy trinity has deceived the nations into believing they can win and conquer. Still, they will receive destruction as a reward for their attempt. The Lord of lords and King of kings is the One who will defeat His enemies. The coalition of nations' armies will be eradicated entirely with just one command from the great sword of His spoken word.

> Then a voice came from the throne, saying, "Praise our God, all you His servants and those who fear Him, both small and great!"
>
> And I heard, as it were, the voice of a great multitude, as the sound of many waters and as the sound of mighty thunderings, saying, "Alleluia! For the Lord God Omnipotent reigns! Let us be glad and rejoice and give Him glory, for the marriage of the Lamb has come, and His wife has made herself ready." And to her it was granted to be arrayed in fine linen, clean and bright, for the fine linen is the righteous acts of the saints.
>
> Then he said to me, "Write: 'Blessed are those who are called to the marriage supper of the Lamb!'" And he said to me, "These are the true sayings of God." And I fell at his feet to worship him. But he said to me, "See that you do not do that! I am your fellow servant, and of your brethren who have the testimony of Jesus. Worship God! For the testimony of Jesus is the spirit of prophecy."
>
> Revelation 19:5–10

A voice from the throne bellows out, "Praise our God, all you His servants and those who fear Him, both small and great!" It is the voice of our Lord, and at His command, a great multitude of the heavenly host of angels singing praise breaks out in heaven. They are rejoicing over all the saints, for the marriage of the Lamb has come! The bride is ready, the wedding union is here, and a marriage supper is on the horizon! The bride looks radiant in their clean white linen, glowing bright with Christ's righteousness through faith. Their righteousness didn't come from their own works; it is imputed righteousness given to them (and us) by our faith in Jesus Christ. They have run the good race and stayed faithful to the bridegroom, giving glory to our Almighty God! The prayers of the martyred saints we saw in Revelation 6:10 are finally here; their prayer has been answered. All the saints join in with the angelic choir and, in perfect harmony, sing, "Alleluia! For the Lord God Omnipotent reigns!" The time has now come for our glorious Lord Christ to ride into battle with the armies of heaven, the angels, and His saints. He will ride to take back what is rightfully His. All the world will see the glory of the coming Son of Man! He will usher in His kingdom and make all things right again!

Now I saw heaven opened, and behold, a white horse. And He who sat on him was called Faithful and True, and in righteousness He judges and makes war. His eyes were like a flame of fire, and on His head were many crowns. He had a name written that no one knew except Himself. He was clothed with a robe dipped in blood, and His name is called The Word of God. And the armies in heaven, clothed in fine linen, white and clean, followed Him on white horses. Now out of His mouth goes a sharp sword, that with it He should strike the nations. And He Himself will rule them with a rod of iron. He Himself treads the winepress of the fierceness and wrath of Almighty God. And He has on His robe and on His thigh a name written:

KING OF KINGS AND LORD OF LORDS.

Revelation 19:11–16

In chapter 6 of Revelation, we saw another rider on a white horse who came to conquer the minds and the hearts of the people on earth. He did this to prepare them, for he soon demanded them all to worship him. However, the Rider of this horse is coming to conquer. Still, unlike the son of perdition, the Son of Man reveals Himself as Lord of lords and King of kings, who is faithful and true. This white horse speaks of honor, power, and swiftness. It speaks of victory. Being "called Faithful and True" assures us that He keeps all His promises. The Word of God is faithful. This majestic Rider is both judge and general, and His horse is a horse of war. He comes to judge those who have rejected Him. John F. Walvoord wrote the following:

> All of these passages point to the sad conclusion that in the day of judgment it is too late for men to expect the mercy of God. There is nothing more inflexible than divine judgment where grace has been spurned. The scene of awful judgment which comes from this background is in flat contradiction of the modern point of view that God is dominated entirely by His attribute of love.

Instead of demanding and coercing people to worship Him as the antichrist had done, people will fall and worship Jesus because He is worthy. They will know He is God when He comes in His glory, and all will see Him. His description instills awe and wonder in all who read it. It invokes a fear of the Lord and an overwhelming gratitude that you are His own. You feel grateful that you belong to Him and are unlike those who have worshipped the beast. He doesn't come now as He first did, helpless, humble, and submissive, to take our place on the cross. Now Jesus comes riding in as the avenging Lord in all His majestic glory! The all-powerful Leader of righteous saints, angelic armies, and Ruler over all things. His eyes were like a flame of fire, and on His head were many crowns. His eyes burn like fire to sear into the hearts of men to discern their secrets. He knows the motives that lie in the hearts of humanity. C.H. Spurgeon wrote,

> There are no secrets here that Christ does not see. There is no lewd thought, there is no unbelieving skepticism, that Christ does not read. There is no hypocrisy, no formalism, no deceit, that he does not scan as easily as a man reads a page in a book. His eyes are like a flame of fire to read us through and through and know us to our inmost soul.

The crown Jesus wore on the earth at His first advent was a crown of thorns, but this time, He wears many crowns, which are crowns of royalty and ultimate authority. The fact that there are many denotes His supremacy in that authority and power. As King of kings, He has unlimited sovereignty. "He was clothed with a robe dipped in blood, and His name is called The Word of God" (Revelation 19:13). The apostle John wrote about Jesus as being the Word of God (John 1:1–3). He was with God, and He was God in the beginning. Some Bible scholars think His robe being "dipped in blood" could be His own blood reminding us of the cross, but I believe because of the prophecy of Isaiah 63:3–4, it is the blood of His enemies slain. "And the armies in heaven, clothed in fine linen, white and clean, followed Him on white horses" (Revelation 19:14). Angels will certainly be coming with Jesus, but the focus here is on His saints who will follow Him into battle on white horses, wearing their only armor: white and clean fine linen, their righteousness. "Now out of His mouth goes a sharp sword, that with it He should strike the nations" (Revelation 19:15). The sword represents the power of His word. As He spoke the heavens and the earth into existence, He can also destroy with the spoken word from His mouth.

"And He Himself will rule them with a rod of iron" (Revelation 19:15). He will establish His perfect government, the kingdom on earth, where He'll rule and reign with a "rod of iron." "He Himself treads the winepress of the fierceness and wrath of Almighty God." Again, this parallels the prophet Isaiah's "winepress" in chapter 63 of the book of Isaiah. This last verse proclaims His sovereignty over the earth, its people, and all its creatures. "And He has on His robe and on His thigh a name written: KING OF KINGS AND LORD OF LORDS" (Revelation 19:16). He alone is the sovereign Lord over the earth. He will be the reigning King over all the world once He returns. Joseph Seiss writes,

> It does not mean the leavening of existing governments with Christian principles, the spiritual conversion of countries and empires, leaving them in existence, and simply Christianizing them so as to exhibit something of Christ's spirit in their administrations; but the total displacement of all this world's sovereigns and governments, the taking of all dominion and authority out of their hands and putting it in the hands of Christ, as the true and only King of the world.

Jesus is coming to bring an end to man's rebellion against God. Many people on the earth will gather to bring war against the Lord Jesus at His coming. The armies of the world's nations will blanket the Middle East from Israel to Edom. They will gather in the Jezreel Valley near the town of Megiddo. This unheavenly militia, led by the antichrist, who in turn is ruled by Satan, will probably number into the hundreds of millions, similar in number to the armies we saw in Revelation 9:16. They believe with such an immense horde of trained soldiers, ready to make war, that they can't possibly lose. But the King of kings is coming to "trample the wine vat." He will stand against these forces, and He will prevail.

> Then I saw an angel standing in the sun; and he cried with a loud voice, saying to all the birds that fly in the midst of heaven, "Come and gather together for the supper of the great God, that you may eat the flesh of kings, the flesh of captains, the flesh of mighty men, the flesh of horses and of those who sit on them, and the flesh of all people, free and slave, both small and great."

> And I saw the beast, the kings of the earth, and their armies, gathered together to make war against Him who sat on the horse and against His army. Then the beast was captured, and with him the false prophet who worked signs in his presence, by which he deceived those who received the mark of the beast and those who worshiped his image. These two were cast alive into the lake of fire burning with brimstone. And the rest were killed with the sword which proceeded from the mouth of Him who sat on the horse. And all the birds were filled with their flesh.

> Revelation 19:17–21

In preparation for the great battle, the angel standing in the sun calls forth to all the fowl of the earth to gather and feed. He calls on them to feed on the flesh of all who will shortly succumb to the swift ferocity of the avenging Lord. During this time in the tribulation, no matter what your station in life is, if you are part of this rebellion against God, you will perish by the spoken word of the Lord. "And I saw the beast, the kings of the earth, and their armies, gathered together to make war against Him who sat on the horse and against His army." It is delusional that Satan, the antichrist, and their followers believe they could ever come against the returning Lord and be victorious. The folly of man's rebellion against God has no bounds. Because of satanic influence on humankind along with humanity's fallen flesh in this cursed world, man has always had an element of enmity against God. Humanity has rebelled and fought against every notion of a Creator since the fall of man. Those who are rebellious have steadfastly set themselves against God and refused to believe they need Him. This spirit of the antichrist had existed since Genesis 3:15 when God laid out His plan to save humanity from sin. Genesis 3:15, referred to by some Bible scholars as the Protoevangelium, was the first mention of the gospel written in the Holy Bible. The word "Protoevangelium" combines two Greek words: *protos* means "first," and *evangelion* means "good news" or "gospel." *Evangelion* is the Greek word from which our modern word "evangelism" is derived. Still, despite man's rebellion, God calls everyone to Himself. Some will hear the calling, and some will not. God knows who will respond to His grace and those who will refuse. He knows who will love the Lord and follow Him and those who will choose Satan and the world. Those who have rejected to worship their Creator have gathered together here in a vast multitude to come up against God in their worship of the antichrist. Many are unaware they are worshipping Satan because of strong delusion. By this last-ditch effort to rid the world of Jesus, they will mindlessly go forth into the battle of Armageddon, and in the blink of an eye, they will be no more.

In these last verses of chapter 19, John wrote nothing about an actual battle, simply because there was no battle. It was more like the immediate destruction of this substantial and vast militia, all at once in a single moment. It was all Jesus; these armies didn't fire a shot. Such is the power of our Almighty God! Donald Grey Barnhouse commented on this: "The battle of Armageddon is the laughter of God against the climax of man's arrogance."

This engagement will be a swift act of divine judgment rather than a prolonged battle. It will be over and done before the armies of the antichrist ever realize it's started. In quick succession, the antichrist and the false prophet will be captured and cast alive into the burning lake of fire, and then "the rest were killed with the sword which proceeded from the mouth of Him who sat on the horse." With just one word from the Lord, the conflict was over.

> Then I saw an angel coming down from heaven, having the key to the bottomless pit and a great chain in his hand. He laid hold of the dragon, that serpent of old, who is the Devil and Satan, and bound him for a thousand years; and he cast him into the bottomless pit, and shut him up, and set a seal on him, so that he should deceive the nations no more till the thousand years were finished. But after these things he must be released for a little while.
>
> And I saw thrones, and they sat on them, and judgment was committed to them. Then I saw the souls of those who had been beheaded for their witness to Jesus and for the word of God, who had not worshiped the beast or his image, and had not received his mark on their foreheads or on their

hands. And they lived and reigned with Christ for a thousand years. But the rest of the dead did not live again until the thousand years were finished. This is the first resurrection. Blessed and holy is he who has part in the first resurrection. Over such the second death has no power, but they shall be priests of God and of Christ, and shall reign with Him a thousand years.

Revelation 20:1–6

Previously, in chapter 9 of the book of Revelation, when the fifth angel sounded his trumpet, we first heard about the "bottomless pit" or the "abyss," as translated in Greek. When the fifth trumpet sounded, the angel took the key to the bottomless pit and opened it up, releasing the demonic locusts onto the world. In Revelation 20:1, the Lord uses an angel to cast Satan into the bottomless pit. He will remain bound for a thousand years until he is released briefly at the end of the millennial kingdom. The name "Satan" means "adversary." He has been called various names since he tempted Eve and caused man's fall six thousand years ago. "Serpent" was what he was referred to when he enticed Eve to eat the fruit from the forbidden tree. The "devil" is another common term for our evil adversary, and it means "accuser or slanderer."

In the book of Revelation, we've seen him referred to as a "dragon." However, regardless of what one calls him, he is the fallen angel, Lucifer, created by God, who rebelled against Him and persuaded other angels to join with him in his hatred for God and man. He and his demons have plagued humanity during his dominion over the earth, which was given to him when Adam sinned against God, relinquishing man's dominion over the earth and handing it to Satan. Humanity, the earth, and all the creatures in it were cursed with sin when man believed Satan's lies instead of God's truth. The adversary Satan has held dominion over the earth up until now. But now Jesus has returned to redeem His purchased possession that He paid for on the cross. Dominion and sovereignty belong to Christ, the Lord and King. Satan, now bound, is no longer the prince of the air, and humanity will no longer be under the sway and influence of his evil temptations. Jesus now rules the earth, while he who was overcome is banished to the abyss for a thousand years. God's will being done on earth even as it is in heaven. John sees the saints of the church age, those who had been raptured or resurrected before the wrath, sitting on their thrones. He saw the martyred saints around the throne with their Lord, who'd been martyred during the tribulation, now at peace in their souls. Peace instead of war will now be prevalent upon the earth.

Mankind and the creatures of the earth will now live in harmony with each other. No longer will the beasts of the earth eat meat. They will eat hay and no longer kill for their food. The earth will return to the beauty of the garden of Eden, it will be a perfect climate, and the earth will no longer convulse in birth pangs travailing in anticipation of its restoration. The trees and plants will flourish, and rivers will flow to the east, the west, the north, and the south, stemming from the throne in Jerusalem to provide all the earth with fresh water. Nations will thrive and grow and not be plagued by anything or anyone because the Lord will rule with an iron rod. The only remaining people on earth will be those resurrected and those still in their mortal bodies. God does not tempt anyone into sin, so now that Satan is bound, if sin exists, it will originate from the carnal flesh of mortal men.

The immortals will rule on earth along with Christ, our King of kings. Sadly, during the millennium, sin will still draw mortal men away from righteousness, and the devil, once he is released after a thousand years, will easily persuade men to rebel against God once more. The world won't be perfect until after the millennium when God ushers the earth and us into the Eternal. But during the millennium, it will be a far better world than we know today. After the thousand-year reign of Christ, God will create a new heaven and a new earth. One day, the earth will be purified by fire, and the heavenly city of Jerusalem will descend from heaven to rest upon the renewed earth. There, God will dwell with His children and the angels forever, and sin will never exist again. After Satan is bound at the beginning of the millennium, it will be a time to rejoice and celebrate. But as time passes and new generations are born, sin will again become prevalent. Corruptible men will still be sinful creatures and have to pay the consequences of their evil ambitions.

In Matthew chapter 25, Jesus told us when He returns in His glory to pour out His wrath, He will judge the nations who came against Israel. He will separate the sheep (those who are righteous) from the goats (those who are wicked). The "sheep" have received Jesus Christ as Lord and Savior and helped Israel. The "goats" are those who have rejected Jesus Christ, God's gift of salvation, and came against Israel. The "sheep" will enter the kingdom of God, and the "goats" will be condemned to the lake of fire for eternal torment simply because they chose not to receive Christ as their Savior and instead decided to persecute God's people. This event is described in Jesus' discourse, as written in Matthew:

> When the Son of Man comes in His glory, and all the holy angels with Him, then He will sit on the throne of His glory. All the nations will be gathered before Him, and He will separate them one from another, as a shepherd divides his sheep from the goats. And He will set the sheep on His right hand, but the goats on the left. Then the King will say to

those on His right hand, "Come, you blessed of My Father, inherit the kingdom prepared for you from the foundation of the world: for I was hungry and you gave Me food; I was thirsty and you gave Me drink; I was a stranger and you took Me in; I was naked and you clothed Me; I was sick and you visited Me; I was in prison and you came to Me."

Then the righteous will answer Him, saying, "Lord, when did we see You hungry and feed You, or thirsty and give You drink? When did we see You a stranger and take You in, or naked and clothe You? Or when did we see You sick, or in prison, and come to You?" And the King will answer and say to them, "Assuredly, I say to you, inasmuch as you did it to one of the least of these My brethren, you did it to Me."

Then He will also say to those on the left hand, "Depart from Me, you cursed, into the everlasting fire prepared for the devil and his angels: for I was hungry and you gave Me no food; I was thirsty and you gave Me no drink; I was a stranger and you did not take Me in, naked and you did not clothe Me, sick and in prison and you did not visit Me."

Then they also will answer Him, saying, "Lord, when did we see You hungry or thirsty or a stranger or naked or sick or in prison, and did not minister to You?" Then He will answer them, saying, "Assuredly, I say to you, inasmuch as you did not do it to one of the least of these, you did not do it to Me." And these will go away into everlasting punishment, but the righteous into eternal life.

Matthew 25:31–46

In summary, God's wrath has been poured out, and the seventieth week of Daniel has ended with Christ as Victor. All of Daniel's prophecies have been fulfilled. God's kingdom on earth has been ushered in by the conquering King and Lord of all the earth. His government of peace on earth has been established and will last for a thousand years. Satan has been restrained and will remain so until the end of the millennium. His release will demonstrate that the human heart is inherently corrupted by sin and that humans cannot be saved simply by their own merit but need divine intervention. Man will still reject God, even after living in His literal presence on earth for a thousand years, because mortal men will be born with the Adamic nature. God has provided the way to end the enmity between Him and us all. But we must choose, as He has bestowed on us all a free will. We have the means to escape the horrors of the tribulation you've just read about. You don't have to read the Bible every day, you don't have to say repetitive prayers, and you don't have to attend church every week to be saved. As Christians, we should do these things to better our relationship with the Lord, but doing them is not the means to salvation or the forgiveness of sin. We are saved by grace alone and not by works. There is no need to do good works to receive it; salvation is a gift from God. We receive salvation through His mercy and grace by our faith in the Lord Jesus Christ.

CHAPTER 11

THE MILLENNIAL KINGDOM AND THE ETERNAL

> And I saw thrones, and they sat on them, and judgment was committed to them. Then I saw the souls of those who had been beheaded for their witness to Jesus and for the word of God, who had not worshiped the beast or his image, and had not received his mark on their foreheads or on their hands. And they lived and reigned with Christ for a thousand years.
>
> Revelation 20:4

In the verses of Isaiah chapters 35 and 65, we find prophecies of life in the coming kingdom, where the Lord will reign. Life in the millennial kingdom on earth will be wonderful for a thousand years! Satan has been bound and will have no power over the earth and its inhabitants during the millennium (Revelation 20:1–3). The curse will be removed from the earth and revitalized by God, reformed to the glorious beauty of the garden before the fall. For a thousand years, man will live and dwell in peace—working, marrying, having children and families. It will be a time of peace; no longer will man make war or fight against each other, for Jesus will be Lord and King on the earth, and He will justly rule and govern the earth with His saints! Wild animals will no longer be a threat to man.

They will eat hay and no longer hunt and kill for food (Isaiah 11:6–8). A child will be able to walk up to a full-grown lion and hug him like he was a puppy! No deformities will exist, for every mortal man will be healed and restored (Isaiah 35:4–6). At one hundred years of age, people will still be young and youthful! It will be drastically different for mortals to live on earth during the millennium because it will be a far greater existence than our life here. The future generations born during the one-thousand-year millennium won't know of any other way of life than the peaceful one they are experiencing because they will have never seen nor lived on the cursed earth that we live on now! On the millennial earth, there will be no more war or oppression from anyone. No poverty or hardship will exist, and love and peace will abound.

> The wilderness and the wasteland shall be glad for them, And the desert shall rejoice and blossom as the rose; It shall blossom abundantly and rejoice, Even with joy and singing. The glory of Lebanon shall be given to it, The excellence of Carmel and Sharon. They shall see the glory of the LORD, The excellency of our God.

> Strengthen the weak hands, And make firm the feeble knees. Say to those who are fearful-hearted, "Be strong, do not fear! Behold, your God will come with vengeance, With the recompense of God; He will come and save you."

> Then the eyes of the blind shall be opened, And the ears of the deaf shall be unstopped. Then the lame shall leap like a deer, And the tongue of the dumb sing. For waters shall burst forth in the wilderness, And streams in the desert. The parched

ground shall become a pool, And the thirsty land springs of water; In the habitation of jackals, where each lay, There shall be grass with reeds and rushes.

A highway shall be there, and a road, And it shall be called the Highway of Holiness. The unclean shall not pass over it, But it shall be for others. Whoever walks the road, although a fool, Shall not go astray. No lion shall be there, Nor shall any ravenous beast go up on it; It shall not be found there. But the redeemed shall walk there, And the ransomed of the LORD shall return, And come to Zion with singing, With everlasting joy on their heads. They shall obtain joy and gladness, And sorrow and sighing shall flee away.

Isaiah 35:1–10

We will all speak the same language in the millennium (Zephaniah 3:9). There will be a beautiful "temple" in the millennium, where the priests will perform sacrifices as a reminder and memorial of the Lord's great sacrifice He made on the cross for the salvation of humanity. You'll find a beautiful description of the millennial temple in Ezekiel, chapters 40–48. These sacrifices will no longer be for the covering of one's sins. Jesus took care of that, once and for all, on the cross at Calvary! During the millennium, the people of the earth will succeed at whatever they do and thrive without any fear of someone stealing what they've earned because Jesus, with the saints, will maintain peace and rule with an "iron rod." The King of kings will not tolerate wickedness and oppression (Revelation 2:27, Revelation 12:5, Revelation 19:15). Those with "mortal" bodies who enter the millennium having survived the tribulation will still have the Adamic nature that believers had before they were resurrected or translated. Mortal men, though Satan is bound (Revelation 20:3), will still be subject to their fleshly desires. If they choose not to receive Jesus during the millennium, they will be cursed to not live beyond one hundred years. The cursed will be those people who reject their Lord and King Jesus and rebel, not wanting to obey God, and will die when they reach one hundred years old. All will know of this, so none will have any excuse for blaming God. He will be fair and loving as always, and people will clearly understand the consequences of making the right choice. If they accept Christ Jesus, they will live on beyond their hundred years. Mortal men, in Christ, will live for hundreds of years, much like the people did in Genesis in the Old Testament. Humanity, the earth, and all its creatures will be in perfect harmony with God again, just as in the garden of Eden.

> But be glad and rejoice forever in what I create; For behold, I create Jerusalem as a rejoicing, And her people a joy. I will rejoice in Jerusalem, And joy in My people; The voice of weeping shall no longer be heard in her, Nor the voice of crying.

> "No more shall an infant from there live but a few days, Nor an old man who has not fulfilled his days; For the child shall die one hundred years old, But the sinner being one hundred years old shall be accursed. They shall build houses and inhabit them; They shall plant vineyards and eat their fruit. They shall not build and another inhabit; They shall not plant and another eat; For as the days of a tree, so shall be the days of My people, And My elect shall long enjoy the work of their hands. They shall not labor in vain, Nor bring forth children for trouble; For they shall be the descendants of the blessed of the LORD, And their offspring with them.

"It shall come to pass That before they call, I will answer; And while they are still speaking, I will hear. The wolf and the lamb shall feed together, The lion shall eat straw like the ox, And dust shall be the serpent's food. They shall not hurt nor destroy in all My holy mountain," Says the LORD.

Isaiah 65:18–25

People will no longer be punished for the iniquities of their ancestors; everyone will be held accountable for their sins only (Jeremiah 31:29–30). Every mortal will have the opportunity to choose Jesus. However, some still will not do so in the millennium, even though Jesus and the saints will be right here on earth with them! During the millennium, God has established that the "Immortals" will rule over the "Mortals." It will be the job of the ambassadors, kings, and priests to Christ (the saints) to govern and rule over the people on earth. They will rule in peace with Christ the King during the millennial kingdom. This will continue until the new heaven and the new earth are established after the one-thousand-year reign. Toward the end of the thousand-year reign, Jesus will release Satan from the bottomless pit for a short time (Revelation 20:7). Satan will be able to incite many mortals to turn against Jesus. The nations will make war (Gog and Magog) and come against Jesus and His saints (Revelation 20:8). They will lose the battle because God will instantly destroy them with fire from the heavens (Revelation 20:9). The reason Satan is loosed again at this time is to prove sin is evil and powerful, and eternal punishment is a necessity. It shows that God is just and long-suffering toward His creation, but sin must always be dealt with eventually.

"He shall judge between the nations, And rebuke many people; They shall beat their swords into plowshares, And their spears into pruning hooks; Nation shall not lift up sword against nation, Neither shall they learn war anymore" (Isaiah 2:4).

We've seen a glimpse of what mortal life on earth will be like during the millennium; however, as members of "the body of Christ" (the church), it is encouraging to consider how life will be for us, the glorified saints of Christ. Well, it will be a time of newness and wonder as we marvel at the beauty of God's creation all around us. Still, unlike the mortals during the millennium, we will have some eternal gifts from God, which will be something to marvel at! It all starts for us, who are already saved when the rapture takes place! Once we are "transformed" at the rapture, we will have an imperishable, incorruptible, and glorified body with the same capabilities as Jesus' body had after His resurrection! (1 Thessalonians 4:13–17, 1 Corinthians 15:52–53).

During the tribulation, for individuals who were saved but passed away before Jesus' return, their souls will ascend to heaven, and their bodies will rest in the grave. Upon Jesus' return at the end of the tribulation, their bodies will be resurrected and reunited with their souls, similar to the believers during the rapture (Revelation 20:4). What happens after God's saints follow Jesus back to earth? What is the status of the church, Jesus' bride, during God's wrath on earth? During the tribulation on earth, the church has been in heaven. Jesus called them from the earth, taking them to the heavenly realm with Him after joining Him in the air. As Jesus returns to earth to redeem it to Himself, the Lord's glorified saints will be with Him. They've seen the city of heaven (yes, heaven is a city, and a very large one), they've stood before the "Bema Seat" and received their rewards (crowns) for the good they have done. The "bride" has joined Jesus at the "marriage of the Lamb," feasting and celebrating with the Lord at "the marriage supper of the Lamb," and now are about to follow the Lord Jesus back to Earth, leaving the heavenly realm behind.

In Acts 8:38–40, Phillip is caught away by the spirit of the Lord. He immediately traveled from where he baptized the eunuch to the city of Azotus, several miles away. That's what we'll able to do in our glorified bodies: to travel from one place to another, even great distances, in a moment! Our new glorified body will be able to move from the physical realm to the spiritual realm, just like Jesus' can. Remember, you will be Christ's ambassadors to the earth and need these capabilities to perform your new duties! If you think life with Jesus will be boring, you are mistaken. Once we join with Jesus, our eternal lives will be filled with wonder and awe that we can't even begin to imagine in these bodies we have now! We will experience life as we never have before.

We have a beautiful glimpse of what will occur in the millennial kingdom and beyond, as written down in the Scriptures! Let's look at what our new glorified bodies will be like in the kingdom. We'll start by seeing in Scripture what Jesus' body was like, following His resurrection, because our bodies will be transformed to be like His.

> For our citizenship is in heaven, from which we also
> eagerly wait for the Savior, the Lord Jesus Christ,
> who will transform our lowly body that it may be
> conformed to His glorious body, according to the
> working by which He is able even to subdue all
> things to Himself.

> Philippians 3:20–21

"Now it came to pass, as He sat at the table with them, that He took bread, blessed and broke it, and gave it to them. Then their eyes were opened and they knew Him; and He vanished from their sight" (Luke 24:30–31).

"Now as they said these things, Jesus Himself stood in the midst of them, and said to them, 'Peace to you.' But they were terrified and frightened, and supposed they had seen a spirit"

(Luke 24:36–37).

> "Behold My hands and My feet, that it is I Myself.
> Handle Me and see, for a spirit does not have flesh
> and bones as you see I have." When He had said
> this, He showed them His hands and His feet. But
> while they still did not believe for joy, and marveled,
> He said to them, "Have you any food here?" So they
> gave Him a piece of a broiled fish and some hon-
> eycomb. And He took it and ate in their presence.
>
> Luke 24:39–43

"Then, the same day at evening, being the first day of the week, when the doors were shut where the disciples were assembled, for fear of the Jews, Jesus came and stood in the midst, and said to them, 'Peace be with you'" (John 20:19).

> And after eight days His disciples were again inside,
> and Thomas with them. Jesus came, the doors be-
> ing shut, and stood in the midst, and said, "Peace to
> you!" Then He said to Thomas, "Reach your finger
> here, and look at My hands; and reach your hand
> here, and put it into My side. Do not be unbeliev-
> ing, but believing."
>
> John 20:26–27

We are told in Scripture that we will have a body like Jesus, and as seen in the above scriptures, Jesus vanished instantly after breaking bread with His disciples. Then they went to Jerusalem and told the other disciples what they had seen, and then suddenly Jesus stood in the midst of them. He had them touch Him to show He was flesh and bone, and then He ate with them to show He could eat in His resurrected body. Then, on two other occasions, He appeared suddenly in their midst.

He had Thomas put his hand into His wounds from the crucifixion to show He wasn't a disembodied spirit. Thus, Jesus had a very physical body, could move through solid objects, and travel instantly from one place to another. Yet, He could still eat and drink as someone with flesh and bone. His resurrected body is the same type of body we will have when resurrected, glorified, and living in the millennial kingdom! All of this comes to us by our trust and faith in Jesus Christ!

> But the day of the Lord will come as a thief in the night, in which the heavens will pass away with a great noise, and the elements will melt with fervent heat; both the earth and the works that are in it will be burned up. Therefore, since all these things will be dissolved, what manner of persons ought you to be in holy conduct and godliness, looking for and hastening the coming of the day of God, because of which the heavens will be dissolved, being on fire, and the elements will melt with fervent heat? Nevertheless we, according to His promise, look for new heavens and a new earth in which righteousness dwells.

> 2 Peter 3:10–13

> But the heavens and the earth which are now preserved by the same word, are reserved for fire until the day of judgment and perdition of ungodly men.

> But, beloved, do not forget this one thing, that with the Lord one day is as a thousand years, and a thousand years as one day. The Lord is not slack concerning His promise, as some count slackness, but is longsuffering toward us, not willing that any

should perish but that all should come to repentance.

2 Peter 3:7–9

"For behold, I create new heavens and a new earth; And the former shall not be remembered or come to mind" (Isaiah 65:17).

During the millennial reign of Christ, our existence for a thousand years, as citizens of heaven, will be on the earth following the tribulation, while heaven remains in the heavenly realm, with God the Father on the throne. The millennial kingdom is not the final destination where we will spend eternity. At "the great white throne judgment," all those who have rejected Christ and died in their sins will be judged, and a "new earth" will be formed. This new earth will be cleansed by fire and regenerated anew, after which heaven will come down from the spiritual realm by the power of God. This is the heavenly city of Jerusalem, a "new heaven" that will rest on the earth, where God and the Lamb will reside seated on the throne. All the saints and angels will live together with God Almighty and the Lamb within the heavenly city.

> Now I saw a new heaven and a new earth, for the first heaven and the first earth had passed away. Also there was no more sea. Then I, John, saw the holy city, New Jerusalem, coming down out of heaven from God, prepared as a bride adorned for her husband. And I heard a loud voice from heaven saying, "Behold, the tabernacle of God is with men, and He will dwell with them, and they shall be His people. God Himself will be with them and be their God. And God will wipe away every tear from their eyes; there shall be no more death, nor sorrow, nor crying.

There shall be no more pain, for the former things have passed away."

Then He who sat on the throne said, "Behold, I make all things new." And He said to me, "Write, for these words are true and faithful."

And He said to me, "It is done! I am the Alpha and the Omega, the Beginning and the End. I will give of the fountain of the water of life freely to him who thirsts. He who overcomes shall inherit all things, and I will be his God and he shall be My son. But the cowardly, unbelieving, abominable, murderers, sexually immoral, sorcerers, idolaters, and all liars shall have their part in the lake which burns with fire and brimstone, which is the second death."

Revelation 21:1–8

In the first eight verses of Revelation chapter 21, John sees a "new heaven" and a "new earth." John has described the "new earth" as no longer having any sea. Whether that means the oceans of the old earth or a population description is speculative. Earlier in Revelation, the word "sea" or "seas" was used to describe multitudes of people, like we would describe a considerable crowd as a "sea of people." If it is taken figuratively, it means there won't be such a thing as Gentile nations. If taken literally, it means there will be no oceans. However, there will be lakes and rivers. We will have to wait and see this after we get there. He then describes the holy city, descending out of heaven from God, and beautifully dressed as a "bride," as his prophetic sight gives him further revelation from Jesus Christ. He hears a loud voice from the throne saying, "Behold, the tabernacle of God is with men, and He will dwell with them"

(Revelation 21:3). Dwelling among His creation has been God's plan all along. When He created mankind, it was for us all to live with Him, for His pleasure, and to bless us with His presence in paradise for all eternity. We are told there will be no more death, mourning, crying, or pain in the new heaven and earth, as the old order of things has passed away. It will truly be a wonderful paradise in the presence of the Almighty God! Jesus then speaks to John (and us all) from the throne and says He is making everything new. He tells John to write down these words, "for these words are true and faithful." He declares, "It is done," similarly to what He said on the cross just before giving up His life for us when He said, "It is finished" (John 19:30). He declares He is God Almighty, "the Alpha and the Omega," and gives freely from the spring of the "water of life" to all who are thirsty, with no cost. He basically tells us He is available to all who seek to find Him, and our salvation is a gift, not to be earned. Those who are "victorious" in Christ will inherit all, but those who reject Christ will "have their part in the lake which burns with fire and brimstone, which is the second death."

> Then one of the seven angels who had the seven bowls filled with the seven last plagues came to me and talked with me, saying, "Come, I will show you the bride, the Lamb's wife." And he carried me away in the Spirit to a great and high mountain, and showed me the great city, the holy Jerusalem, descending out of heaven from God, having the glory of God. Her light was like a most precious stone, like a jasper stone, clear as crystal. Also she had a great and high wall with twelve gates, and twelve angels at the gates, and names written on them, which are the names of the twelve tribes of the children of Israel: three gates on the east, three

gates on the north, three gates on the south, and three gates on the west.

Now the wall of the city had twelve foundations, and on them were the names of the twelve apostles of the Lamb. And he who talked with me had a gold reed to measure the city, its gates, and its wall. The city is laid out as a square; its length is as great as its breadth. And he measured the city with the reed: twelve thousand furlongs. Its length, breadth, and height are equal. Then he measured its wall: one hundred and forty-four cubits, according to the measure of a man, that is, of an angel. The construction of its wall was of jasper; and the city was pure gold, like clear glass. The foundations of the wall of the city were adorned with all kinds of precious stones: the first foundation was jasper, the second sapphire, the third chalcedony, the fourth emerald, the fifth sardonyx, the sixth sardius, the seventh chrysolite, the eighth beryl, the ninth topaz, the tenth chrysoprase, the eleventh jacinth, and the twelfth amethyst. The twelve gates were twelve pearls: each individual gate was of one pearl. And the street of the city was pure gold, like transparent glass.

Revelation 21:9–21

Now, in these verses, we are again shown a beautiful picture of the heavenly Jerusalem as it descends from heaven. The angel tells John in his vision, "Come, I will show you the bride, the Lamb's wife," as John sees the immense and beautiful city of heaven coming down to the earth. It is referred to as "the Lamb's wife" because the church is going to live within the

New Jerusalem. This is also the first time the church has been referred to in scripture as the "Lamb's wife." Prior to this, in the Bible, the church was referred to as "the bride of Christ." The heavenly city of Jerusalem is the residence of God and the Lamb, the Lamb's wife (His saints), and the angels for all eternity. It is the eternal "new heaven" created by God and the "new earth" it will rest upon! It is brilliant in its beauty, for it reflects the splendor and beauty of God's radiant glory that illuminates it! It is adorned with fine jewels, pearls, and stones of every color. The city and streets are fashioned with transparent gold, purer than was ever known on earth, to allow God's glorious light to shine through and sparkle like the most beautiful diamond. There are twelve gates, each being a single pearl, with an angel at each one to welcome and greet the righteous into the city. On each gate is the name of one of the tribes of Israel as a reminder of the critical role Israel played in humanity's salvation. There is no temple because God will dwell amongst us without any barriers. It is the eternal heaven, a city for all the righteous to dwell in for all time, in the presence of the Almighty God!

The heavenly city is fashioned like a cube, and according to the measurements given in the Bible, it will tower 1,400–1,500 miles tall, wide, and deep (12,000 furlongs). To provide you with an idea of the massive size of this heavenly city, it would cover over half of the United States if placed on American soil. The height of our atmosphere is approximately 7 miles, while the height of the new heaven (Jerusalem) will be 1,500 miles. People on earth won't be able to see the top of it, nor its full width or depth, with the naked eye while standing at its base, or even some miles away, because it is as wide and deep as it is tall! It would be like standing on the beach in California and trying to see the east side of Texas from there. The nations (mortals) will walk in its light, and the immortals will bring their righteousness and glory into it! It is the home of the Father, with many mansions, where Jesus went to make a place for us! (John 14:2) In its grandeur, the heavenly city will be able to house millions upon millions of God's saints and angels. It is where we will all dwell as we serve God on the new earth!

> But I saw no temple in it, for the Lord God Almighty and the Lamb are its temple. The city had no need of the sun or of the moon to shine in it, for the glory of God illuminated it. The Lamb is its light. And the nations of those who are saved shall walk in its light, and the kings of the earth bring their glory and honor into it. Its gates shall not be shut at all by day (there shall be no night there). And they shall bring the glory and the honor of the nations into it. But there shall by no means enter it anything that defiles, or causes an abomination or a lie, but only those who are written in the Lamb's Book of Life.

> Revelation 21:22–27

There will be no night there, for His glory will shine throughout the city and bring light upon the earth, and the city's gates will not be shut by day! He then tells us that the righteous in Christ will have access to the city, bringing "the glory and honor [of the nations] into it." Still, those who reject Christ and hold on to their sin will never have entrance to the heavenly city, "only those who are written in the Lamb's Book of Life." This city is the future heaven that we will all finally know as home, and we will remain with our Lord and King Jesus forever!

> And he showed me a pure river of water of life, clear as crystal, proceeding from the throne of God

and of the Lamb. In the middle of its street, and on either side of the river, was the tree of life, which bore twelve fruits, each tree yielding its fruit every month. The leaves of the tree were for the healing of the nations. And there shall be no more curse, but the throne of God and of the Lamb shall be in it, and His servants shall serve Him. They shall see His face, and His name shall be on their foreheads. There shall be no night there: They need no lamp nor light of the sun, for the Lord God gives them light. And they shall reign forever and ever.

Then he said to me, "These words are faithful and true." And the Lord God of the holy prophets sent His angel to show His servants the things which must shortly take place.

"Behold, I am coming quickly! Blessed is he who keeps the words of the prophecy of this book."

Now I, John, saw and heard these things. And when I heard and saw, I fell down to worship before the feet of the angel who showed me these things.

Then he said to me, "See that you do not do that. For I am your fellow servant, and of your brethren the prophets, and of those who keep the words of this book. Worship God." And he said to me, "Do not seal the words of the prophecy of this book, for the time is at hand. He who is unjust, let him be unjust still; he who is filthy, let him be filthy still; he who is righteous, let him be righteous still; he who is holy, let him be holy still."

"And behold, I am coming quickly, and My reward is with Me, to give to every one according to his work. I am the Alpha and the Omega, the Beginning and the End, the First and the Last."

Blessed are those who do His commandments, that they may have the right to the tree of life, and may enter through the gates into the city. But outside are dogs and sorcerers and sexually immoral and murderers and idolaters, and whoever loves and practices a lie.

"I, Jesus, have sent My angel to testify to you these things in the churches. I am the Root and the Offspring of David, the Bright and Morning Star."

And the Spirit and the bride say, "Come!" And let him who hears say, "Come!" And let him who thirsts come. Whoever desires, let him take the water of life freely.

For I testify to everyone who hears the words of the prophecy of this book: If anyone adds to these things, God will add to him the plagues that are written in this book; and if anyone takes away from the words of the book of this prophecy, God shall take away his part from the Book of Life, from the holy city, and from the things which are written in this book.

He who testifies to these things says, "Surely I am coming quickly."

Amen. Even so, come, Lord Jesus!

The grace of our Lord Jesus Christ be with you all. Amen.

Revelation 22:1–21

There is an implication in chapter 22 that there might be nations of people outside the walls of the heavenly Jerusalem because of the mention of the "water of life" and the "tree of life" with its leaves for the healing of the nations. It implies that someone will benefit from the healing. However, it needs to be clarified. None of the "saints" nor the "angels" would need healing, for they are eternal and incorruptible, so it is unsure who would need the leaves for healing. Our God is all-capable, and we don't know what else He has planned for the new earth in the future, only what Jesus has revealed to us in this book. It is a mystery, like many mysteries that have been given and revealed throughout history. Some things remain hidden, and we must wait and find out. We are informed in the Scripture that the curse affecting us and all of creation, including the earth, will be removed in the Eternal. There will be no more "curse" or its effects on the new earth. We also are told there will be no darkness, sun, or moon, for God will provide light for the earth and illuminate the city with His glory. The Lord immediately tells us, "These words are faithful and true," probably because the information we've been given has seemed "too good to be true" and phenomenal in its imagery!

It seems undeserving for us in this flesh to think of us as kings and queens reigning and ruling alongside our Lord, but He assures us of the fact. When He spoke to Daniel and told him to seal up the things he'd been given in this prophecy, it was because God knew in Daniel's time that people wouldn't understand the meaning. Now, in this verse, He tells John not to seal up the things of this book because it would make sense to modern-day people as the world approaches the "last days." Many consider the book of Revelation a "sealed book" because it is filled with mysteries. Still, once you've studied the Old Testament prophecies and seen the things happening around us, it becomes more apparent in its literal sense. People tend to "spiritualize" the things written in this book rather than take them literally, and then they become meaningless. In the book of Revelation, some things are symbolic. Still, many passages should be taken literally, and these passages in Revelation chapters 21 and 22 should be. Jesus instructs us not to modify or omit anything from the book, as we should accept it in its original form. He understood that during the "last days," we would have knowledge that the apostles didn't have in their day and age. We today are much more technologically advanced, so Jesus knew His followers in the future would be able to grasp their meaning. He knew Christians would only fully comprehend the words in this book as the "end times" approached.

Since we are currently living in those times, we begin to understand it more clearly. He continues by proclaiming who He is: "the Beginning and the End," "the Alpha and the Omega," and "the Root and the Offspring of David," which declares He is and always will be God and Man. As the "Root," He created David as God, and as His "offspring," He was descended from David as Man. He is both the Creator and the Descendant of David! He declares He is "the Bright and Morning Star," identifying Himself as the One who appears near the end of the great tribulation (the second coming). He then continues and again declares that we who obey Him are the "sheepfold," to whom the gates of the heavenly city are open, and that those who have rejected Him will be eternally excluded. After warning not to add to these things or those who do will succumb to the plagues of this book, nor take away from the book, or God shall "take away his part from the Book of Life," the holy city, and from the things written in this book. And He ends with a final promise, "Surely I am coming quickly." Amen.

He who overcomes, I will make him a pillar in the

temple of My God, and he shall go out no more. I will write on him the name of My God and the name of the city of My God, the New Jerusalem, which comes down out of heaven from My God. And I will write on him My new name.

Revelation 3:12

These prophetic promises are our blessed hope and rewards in Christ Jesus, our Lord! Through the revelation of Jesus Christ, we have been shown what it will be like for us, the body of Christ, in the future. God has shown us through His Word, as written in the Scriptures, what we need to know to take hold of this hope! In the Bible, we've only seen a shadow of the glory of the heavenly city and our future eternal lives, but God knew it would be enough for us now, for those who love Him. Here is the reason to choose life that can only be found in Christ Jesus, our Lord and Savior! This "new life" in the new heaven and new earth with the one true living God is the eternal reward we all run the race for since we've come to receive and know Jesus. He Himself is the reward! Through Him come all the blessings of the Father! Praise God for this. Without Jesus, there is nothing to look forward to but eternal suffering and pain. God wants no one to perish. He desires all to come to Him through the gift of His Son, Jesus Christ! He says His yoke is easy, and His burden is light (Matthew 11:30). If you don't know Him yet, choose Jesus Christ today! Receive the Holy Spirit, and begin your walk with Him, knowing your eternal reward is found in Him! You will have a glorious and infinite future to look forward to! It all comes to you when you believe in the work of Jesus Christ, the Son of God, by faith alone.

"In My Father's house are many mansions; if it were not so, I would have told you. I go to prepare a place for you. And if I go and prepare a place for you, I will come again and receive you to Myself; that where I am, there you may be also" (John 14:2–3).

"Looking for the blessed hope and glorious appearing of our great God and Savior Jesus Christ" (Titus 2:13).

EPILOGUE:
CHRIST IS THE ANSWER

God's entire plan for humanity since the fall in the garden of Eden has always been to rescue us, His creation, from the bondage of sin and the wickedness that would permeate the world. God knew before Adam and Eve fell that sin would enter the world. He knew what Satan would do and how it would affect the world for thousands of years to come. God's plan would end all sin and usher in a new and perfect world that would culminate when God creates a new heaven and earth at the close of the coming millennial kingdom. After the great white throne judgment, we will enter the "Eternal." God's great plan for mankind is clear, as written in the Holy Bible from Genesis to Revelation. God's intent is for none of His creation to be lost. He desires us all to be saved in Christ. We need salvation because we have fallen and are under the curse of sin. Our eternal existence hangs on the truth of His Word.

"All we like sheep have gone astray; We have turned, every one, to his own way; And the LORD has laid on Him the iniquity of us all" (Isaiah 53:6).

The Lord has made Himself known to man through evidence in His creation all around us and instilling Himself in man's conscience through His written Word. By design, He has imparted Himself into men's hearts. He has sent disciples out into the world to spread the gospel. In all these things, humanity has no excuse for not recognizing the one true God as the Creator and Sovereign Lord. Everywhere we look on this beautiful planet God created, we can see His invisible attributes all around us! All that we see, in the creatures filled with life all around us, in the stars and the heavens, and in the beauty of His created earth itself, cries out to us evidence of intelligent design by a Grand Creator. We, mankind, are the product of the Creator God ourselves, our bodies living miracles of intelligent design that no man can duplicate through scientific discovery or any other means!

"For since the creation of the world His invisible attributes are clearly seen, being understood by the things that are made, even His eternal power and Godhead, so that they are without excuse" (Romans 1:20).

God has created each one of us with purpose. Each of us is unique in how we fit into His great plan. Whether we have known our Lord from childhood or whether we cry out to Him in the last few moments of our life here on earth, He will receive a heart of repentance. He knows our hearts, so if we're sincerely repentant in our belief, He will accept us and welcome us to Himself because of His great love, mercy, forgiveness, and grace. His love is everlasting! If you don't know the Lord Jesus today, I encourage all of you to seek Him in faith and begin a lasting relationship with Him! None of us know the number of days we have on this earth. To die without Jesus in our sin will mean separation forever from the one true eternal God. Because of our sins, without Christ, we would have to face judgment for our sins by our merit. We will all fail because we can't atone for our sins without a Penal Substitute, who is without sin. God provided us with a Kinsman Redeemer, Jesus Christ, both God and Man who was without sin. Without Jesus and His sacrifice for us in our place, a person without the Savior will fail, for all have sinned (Isaiah 53:6). Those who reject Christ will be judged guilty of their sin, and they will be cast into the lake of fire for all eternity. It is the harsh truth of our existence as God's creation because man fell into sin in the garden of Eden (Adam and Eve). Due to their disobedience, as the mother and father of all humanity, all who are born into this world are born unto sin, having the curse of the "Adamic nature." God only requires us to acknowledge our sins and realize that we need Him for our salvation. We must then repent and believe in Him, trusting His work on the cross as enough to save us. He is the Creator God and the God of truth, justice, and judgment. But He is also a God of mercy, grace, love, and forgiveness! He is the One who created and breathed life into us and loves us all dearly! He wants us with Him so He can lavish us with His blessings as we love and worship Him, living in the paradise of heaven and walking with Him forever! He hates sin because it separates us from Him! Once we fully trust in Him, Jesus is our hope and future. He sacrificed Himself on the cross so that we could be His and He could be ours in the family of God. His resurrection from death to life assures us of eternal life with Him. None of us can save ourselves. We must only believe and trust in Him for our salvation. We were created to worship our God and dwell with Him forever, but our sin separates us. Our only hope in fulfilling our purpose and receiving eternal life with God is by choosing the Way, the Truth, and the Life. Salvation can only be found in Christ Jesus our Lord. Repent of the world and turn to God. Choose Christ and receive God's eternal love through the gift of His only begotten Son. Through His Son, receive God's infinite love, living in joy and the hope of His coming kingdom!

> For God did not send His Son into the world to condemn the world, but that the world through Him might be saved.

> He who believes in Him is not condemned; but he who does not believe is condemned already, because he has not believed in the name of the only begotten Son of God.

John 3:17

God wants none of His creation to be lost, so He sent a Savior. He has made a way where before there was no way. God became Man to be the perfect, sinless substitute to die in our place. The wages of sin is death, so we are cursed to die for our sins. We all need a "substitutionary sacrifice" without sin to save us from the fate that awaits us all. Jesus was that sacrifice. He finished His work on the cross for our salvation. In Christ, we may have life if we choose to receive Him as Lord and Savior. He died carrying the weight of our sins on His shoulders so we could be forgiven. To reject Christ is to sentence ourselves to the second death, which is eternal torment without Him. Agree with God that you are a sinner who needs a Savior! Jesus tells us, "My yoke is easy and My burden is light" (Matthew 11:30) because He wants us to lay all our cares upon Him. He will carry you through this life as you abide in Him daily! If you haven't already, decide to seek God through Christ Jesus. It is the most critical decision you will ever make in your life.

I hope and pray that this study on the final days has enlightened and encouraged you for the days to come as we approach Daniel's seventieth week, according to the prophecy of God.

"Watch therefore, for you do not know what hour your Lord is coming" (Matthew 24:42).

Thank You, Father in heaven, for the gift of Your only begotten Son, Jesus the Christ, and for the Helper who dwells within me, the Holy Spirit, who grants all at the asking: wisdom, discernment, and understanding of the Word of God. Come, Jesus, come. Your will be done on earth as it is in heaven. Amen.

REFERENCES

Alford, Henry. *The Revelation: The New Testament for English Readers*. Vol. 2, Part 2. London: Rivingtons, 1869.

Barnhouse, Donald Grey. *Revelation: An Expositional Commentary*. Grand Rapids, Michigan: Zondervan, 1982.

Blue Letter Bible. "Bible Text Commentaries by Chuck Smith." Accessed December 12, 2023. https://www.blueletterbible.org/commentaries/smith_chuck.

Blue Letter Bible. "Bible Text Commentaries by David Guzik." Accessed December 12, 2023. https://www.blueletterbible.org/commentaries/guzik_david.

Blue Letter Bible. "Bible Text Commentaries by John Brown." Accessed December 12, 2023. https://www.blueletterbible.org/commentaries/brown_john.

Blue Letter Bible. "Bible Text Commentaries by Matthew Henry." Accessed December 12, 2023. https://www.blueletterbible.org/commentaries/mhc.

Seiss, Joseph A. *The Apocalypse: Lectures on the Book of Revelation*. Grand Rapids, Michigan: Kregel Publications, 1987.

Spurgeon, Charles Haddon. *The Metropolitan Tabernacle Pulpit*. Vol. 7–63. Pasadena, Texas: Pilgrim Publications, 1990.

Spurgeon, Charles Haddon. *The New Park Street Pulpit*. Vol. 1–6. Pasadena, Texas: Pilgrim Publications, 1990.

Tenney, Merrill C. *Interpreting Revelation*. Grand Rapids, Michigan: Eerdmans, 1970. Walvoord, John F. *The*

Rapture Question. Grand Rapids, Michigan: Zonder-van, 1979.

Walvoord, John F. *The Revelation of Jesus Christ*. Chicago: Moody Press, 1966.

Printed in the USA
CPSIA information can be obtained
at www.ICGtesting.com
CBHW032326100224
4133CB00002B/9